Expert in a Year

The Ultimate Table Tennis Challenge

Sam Priestley

&

Ben Larcombe

ISBN: **1515184498**
ISBN-13: **978-1515184492**

CONTENTS

ACKNOWLEDGMENTS

There are loads of people that we would like to thank for their help and advice during the challenge…

Katie Larcombe, Ben's wife, was very loving and supportive despite on occasion seeing Ben so little that she was referred to as the "table tennis widow".

Toby Aldous, Daniel Lim & Anthony Griffiths, Sam's flatmates, put up with a lot of table tennis taking over their kitchen. If you watched any of the videos you probably would have seen them cooking dinner in the background while we played.

Mark Simpson gave Sam a few really great one-to-one coaching sessions, spent hours discussing and planning with us online, and worked with Sam via Skype on his mental training and sports psychology.

Steve Brunskill & Paul Warters have welcome us three times to their camps at Swerve. They provided us with great training and coaching, put us up for the night, and gave Sam plenty of advice regarding fitness and his physical training.

Sherwin Remata gave Sam a brilliant coaching session in March and really improved his ability to brush the ball. He gave him a second one-to-one in August.

Eli Baraty had both of us on one of his training camps at The Harefield Academy where he gave us a really beneficial one-to-one session that helped improve Sam's arm speed, adding some much needed aggression to his forehand.

Katia Mifsud & Mario Genovese looked after Sam while he was in Malta, in May. While there he attended some sessions at the HiTT Academy and did a great one-to-one session with Mario.

Lars Rokkjaer & Nicolai Cok helped us organise our trip to Denmark and both showed a lot of interest in the challenge. All the other coaches on the training camp deserve a mention too, especially Sam's coaches, Per Rosin and Lei Yang.

Eszter Igaz gave Sam a one-to-one session in the kitchen in July.

Stephen Gertsen gave Sam two really useful coaching sessions in July and August.

Will Maybanks and the team of coaches and organisers in Eger, Hungary trained Sam while he attended their camp in August. Thank you for the input you had on his development.

Bob Coull and the other guys at ISH were brilliant and very accommodating.

Joshua Nashed was the go-to person whenever we needed to find a local club for Sam to go to. He knew which clubs were open on which days and gave us plenty of help selecting clubs.

Paul Stimpson wrote about our challenge for Table Tennis England. He was also great at helping us promote the challenge and reach more people.

Larry Hodges shared news from our challenge several times on his table tennis coaching blog.

Matt Hetherington interviewed us for his blog and it was a superb interview with some clearly well thought out questions. Thank you for helping us gain some extra exposure.

Romina Concha featured the challenge on the table tennis news site TableTennista.com and shared our videos.

Dan Seemiller Jr shared our video 'Guy Plays Table Tennis Every Day for a Year' on Reddit in February 2015 and started a tidal wave of views that lead to the Expert in a Year challenge going viral.

I'm sure there are plenty of other people that deserve a mention that we have forgotten. Thanks to all of you for everything you have done to help and encourage us.

Sam Priestley & Ben Larcombe

1
THE BOY WHO COULDN'T THROW A BALL

"I have no special talents. I am only passionately curious." - Albert Einstein

It had all gone wrong. I couldn't continue like this. I had to change. Change or give up. I was dedicating myself to a sport, training hard every day while giving up a huge amount of my free time, but I was getting nowhere. No, I'm not talking about table tennis. I'm talking about rowing.

It had started out great. Three years earlier we had been given the opportunity to take up rowing at school. To entice us, they put on a taster session. We were given oars, packed into boats, and let loose to play around. Lots of splashing, very little moving, and a fair amount of laughter followed. 14-year-old Sam loved it. It was fun, and I was rubbish at hockey, so I signed up.

From there it began to ramp up and slowly people started dropping out. That first session had been so much fun that almost half the year had chosen rowing as their 'games option', but by the first winter the majority had quit. Ahh, the winter. Think about how cold your fingers get just from walking around outside. Now imagine not being allowed to wear gloves and having freezing cold water splashed on you every few strokes. It was miserable, but we assured each other that if we could just hold on until spring, it would become awesome again.

Gradually the weather improved, we settled in, and the messing around in boats turned into much more of a sport. By the beginning of the third year, we were down to just four people. Four out of the original 35 had stuck with it. The training grew to a massive 20 hours every week and we prided ourselves on how hardcore we were, how tough.

But I was falling behind. While my boat mates slowly improved, getting better, faster and stronger, I was barely keeping up. I was killing myself, training every day of every week, but it wasn't enough. Worse, I was being overtaken by some of the younger rowers from the year below. While I was struggling to do the set training, missing a session every week or two, they weren't. Plus, they were going above and beyond, and it was showing. I was spending a lot of my free time on rowing, a sport that I wasn't enjoying and wasn't excelling at. It was the worst of both worlds.

At the back of all of our minds was the dream of someday being able to row for our country; to represent Great Britain. I could go to trials, but there was a requirement; you needed to be able to get a sub 7-minute 2k time on the rowing machine. It was time to make a choice; either put in the extra work to try and reach that goal, or give up.

I hatched a plan. The summer holidays were approaching, a time when everyone would slack off, that is everyone except me. Eager and excited I convinced my coach to let me borrow one of the school's rowing machines for the break. I promised myself I would train every day and train hard. I would get that sub 7 minute 2k, even if it killed me.

But I didn't. I failed.

Not only did I fail, but I didn't even manage to stick to my daily regime. The first week started well but pretty quickly I descended into training when I felt 'in the mood', and as a 2k on a rowing machine is a horrible experience, that wasn't very often. My daily training soon turned into every other day, and by the end of the holiday I was only doing a session or two a week. On the first day back at school, I went to the coach and nervously told him I was quitting. I thought he would be upset, but instead he just looked at me with disappointment and replied: *"That's what I expected"*. I haven't been in a rowing boat since.

What happened? Why did I fail? Was it a lack of motivation? A lack of passion, skill or understanding of the sport? Or just bad genes?

If you had asked my coach, a 6 ft 10 monster, he probably would have told you I didn't have the genes. My mother, on the other hand, is pretty convinced I can do whatever I put my mind to. "You just didn't really want it", she'd say. In some respects, both those reasons are just excuses. At the time when friends asked me why I'd quit I had other excuses. I would tell them it was because I wasn't tall enough or that I'd hurt my back and the physio had told me to stop. Both were true, but they weren't the real reasons either.

I quit because I failed my challenge, and I failed my challenge because it was a half-arsed attempt right from the beginning. I'm telling you about it now, but at the time I told no one; I didn't even tell my coach why I wanted to borrow the rowing machine. I didn't want to attempt something and then have to admit I'd failed. Thinking back, as soon as it got tough I slacked off. But why? I think it was to protect myself from failure. "Well, I didn't really try my hardest", I could say to myself. "If I had given it everything I wouldn't have failed. Am I bothered?"

But what would have happened if I'd stuck with it,

rather than giving up when failure looked likely? Would I have rowed for my country? Maybe... maybe not. But would I have been a better rower by the end of it? Certainly.

****

Do you remember that really sporty kid at school? The one who just seemed to be great at everything; awesome at football, a natural at tennis, fast at running. That wasn't me. I was a pretty normal kid; I enjoyed sport, running around, fighting and competition. I liked winning and I didn't like losing.

My parents were pretty typical. They devoured books on how to raise a child and taught me what they value; what they thought would make me the most rounded individual. One of the things early-development books like to talk about is the ABCs of physical literacy and my parents didn't neglect this side of my education. I remember having basketball parties, I used to run around a lot and I was always climbing on things. I learnt to cycle without stabilisers at the age of four, and for the next ten years our family outings were all long bicycle rides.

But neither of my parents are particularly 'sporty' themselves and it seems a few key skills slipped through the net. I didn't learn how to throw a ball, how to kick a football, how to jump and land properly, or how to run correctly. If they themselves didn't know how to do these things how could they teach me? I didn't learn them as a young child, and after that I quickly got to an age where I 'should' at least be proficient. An age where it's embarrassing if you don't have them.

Take football for example. I *never* play football - why? It's not that I don't enjoy it, it's because I don't like feeling like a fool. Whenever I play football I am so bad at it I tend to walk off or just stand at the back, trying to avoid the ball. I can barely kick it in a straight line! What do kids do during lunchtime, every day from the age of 8 to 18? They play football. That is everyone except those of us who were too bad to play. By the time I reached 18 I had played hardly any football, our nation's most popular pastime (although maybe that's Facebook nowadays) and I'd barely got involved at all. I have no idea how much football the average person has played, but it's thousands of hours more than me. No wonder I look so clumsy.

What happens when you're 14 years old and someone asks you to throw them a ball, and you wildly miss? Everyone laughs at you and you never want to throw anyone a ball again. I went through about eight years when I would always throw people stuff underarm because there was a chance they would laugh at me if I did a rubbish overarm throw. But that means that while I'm avoiding practicing these skills, I'm never going to get any better. It's never going to not be embarrassing. I'm never going to be good enough to join in.

It's easy enough for me now to theorise about why I struggled with certain sports, but at the time all I knew was that that was the way of the world and there was nothing I could do about it. I do really enjoy sport and luckily there are sports that don't rely so much on these fundamental coordination skills which I was able to naturally gravitate towards. I have tried rock climbing, shooting, and archery. They all had one thing in common - the key skills aren't taught to many people at a young age. Most people give them a go as they get older.

An even better example is rowing. The skills you require to be good at rowing are ones you never learn until you get in a boat. No one gets into a rowing boat for the first time and can naturally beat someone who has been practicing and taught proper technique for even just a few weeks. Most people, sat in a single boat and told to race, would just capsize.

After rowing, I didn't do much sport until university

when I took up running; but not competitive running. I used to go and do a 5K run on the running machine every day for about 8 months. Every day for 8 months! Almost every time I would get faster. It was awesome; direct results. I wasn't comparing my improvement to anyone else and nobody could see or judge what I was doing. I was just getting personal bests each and every day. I went from stumbling through a 5K run in 28 minutes, to blitzing through it in a very respectable 19.

Then I got injured. As anyone who is into running will tell you, it was probably inevitable. Apparently you're not meant to push your body like that every day. The physio told me I'd never be able to run that fast again, but it had really sparked an interest. After my failure at rowing and a lifetime of being bad at football, it was a real eye-opener. If I could go from being a podgy, below average runner, to being one of the fastest people I knew, what else is possible?

One sport that most people have never played much of is table tennis. Sure, everybody has played but very few go beyond the mucking about stage. In 2013, I went on an out-of-season, mid-week holiday with my flatmates to Tenerife. The place was deserted with literally nothing to do but play table tennis on this slightly damp, dirty outdoor table. We were all rubbish, but it was fun and by the end of the few days we were there, we had got very competitive. Toby was the best, but Dan and I didn't feel that far behind.

We enjoyed it so much that when we got home we purchased a table tennis table which we could just about cram into our communal kitchen/living room. I thought that we'd quickly catch up with Toby, but it didn't happen. We were all improving, but he somehow managed to maintain his lead.

Toby put his dominance down to the quick reactions he'd picked up from being a goalkeeper while at school. I would hardly ever beat him. We'd play ten games and he'd win nine, and nothing I was doing seemed to help. "You need to stop trying to hit the ball so hard", he would say. But how could I improve if I didn't go for shots? I kept thinking that if he keeps playing slow and conservative eventually I'll just be able to smash the ball past him, but it never happened. Was it literally just the goalkeeping experience that set him apart, or was there something about him that made him inherently better than me?

At the same time Toby, Dan and I were busy competing inexpertly in our kitchen, my friend Ben Larcombe, who happened to be a professional table tennis coach, was coming up with a challenge. A challenge where he would intensively train an adult novice in the skills of table tennis in order to dispel a myth that was haunting the sport; the commonly held belief that you could only absorb the correct technique if you started learning at a very young age. The misconception that adults were "too old" to get any good. This would eventually become 'The Expert in a Year Challenge' and my competitive desire to beat Toby combined with my recently formed belief in the power of practice, would make me the perfect guinea pig.

2
THE FORMATION OF THE CHALLENGE

"Give me a dozen healthy infants, well-formed, and my own specified world to bring them up in and I'll guarantee to take any one at random and train him to become any type of specialist I might select - doctor, lawyer, artist, merchant-chief and, yes, even beggar-man and thief, regardless of his talents, penchants, tendencies, abilities, vocations and the race of his ancestors." - John Watson

I have known Ben for many years, and throughout that time the first thing that springs to mind when I think of him is 'table tennis'. He is seriously into his table tennis.

When we were teenagers we were part of the same close-knit group of friends. We'd all meet up regularly and waste the time away. That is all of us except Ben. It felt like almost every weekend Ben would be off travelling around the country, competing in some table tennis tournament. Although we used to laugh at him for taking it so seriously, we also understood it - he loved playing table tennis.

Then in the summer of 2007 he took it to a new level.

We were both getting ready to go to university. I, a bit of a computer geek, was going to study Computer Science and Ben was preparing to study Geography. Then, just a few weeks before his course was meant to start, he did a u-turn, dropped out, and signed up to a table tennis academy for the next two years.

Sacrificing your weekends to do something you love, that I could understand. But sacrificing your future career to do it? I remember thinking it was a ludicrous decision. Even his ever supportive dad told him:

"You can't just play table tennis forever. You'll have to do something eventually."

By this point Ben had been playing a couple of times a week for almost ten years but, just like with my rowing, he wasn't seeing the results he wanted. The same thing would happen at every junior event he entered; he'd get knocked out in the first or second round by a player who was so unbelievably good that it almost wasn't worth them playing the match. Ben didn't have a hope of winning.

"How could these other boys be so good?" He thought to himself. Could it really be that they were born with these super table tennis abilities that he didn't inherit? That didn't seem very likely. For one, they were quite an odd-looking bunch for super athletes. Some of them were short, but some were really tall. Lots were slim, but a few were quite overweight.

Somewhere along the line Ben decided that these players were simply playing a lot more table tennis than him, and that was the difference. From the sounds of it, they were training almost every single day. It got to the point where Ben was a little embarrassed. "I should be better!" he thought. So just like me with my summer rowing challenge, he made a change. He dropped out of university before it had even started and moved to Grantham Table Tennis Academy, where he would be playing pretty much full-time. Whereas I approached my daily rowing challenge timidly, with little conviction, and without telling anyone, Ben did the opposite. Unlike me, he didn't quit. And unlike me, he got the results.

After just nine months of training Ben's senior England ranking went up from about 450th to 250th, and the other Grantham players were experiencing similar improvement. It was like a conveyer belt. Provided they turned up to training and put in the work, an average 18-year-old player would go in and an exceptional 20-year-old player would come out. It happened every year.

Ben found it fascinating and he came to realise he was just as interested in the learning process behind table tennis, as with the playing itself. After two years at Grantham, he enrolled at Nottingham Trent University to study a degree in Coaching and Sport Science. It was while he was there that ex-table tennis champion Matthew Syed released his book Bounce: The Myth of Talent and the Power of Practice, outlining the 10,000-hour theory. To Ben, everything he had assumed to be true was now being backed up by a book filled with research and plenty of table tennis examples.

The main idea could be summarised as follows:

Experts, in all fields, are made not born. There doesn't appear to be any world-class performers that have achieved expertise without putting in at least 10,000 hours (or ten years) of intense deliberate practice. It is the quantity and quality of this practice that determines who will be exceptional, and talent either doesn't exist or isn't very important.

Ben thrived on these sorts of theories and come dissertation time there was only one topic he was interested in investigating. His dissertation was entitled 'The role of deliberate practice in the development of table tennis expertise', and his own research, once again, backed up the idea that what separates an intermediate player from an expert one is simply lots of practice.

After graduating in 2011, Ben started coaching table tennis full-time in a number of schools in London. He was convinced that with enough practice any of his players could experience success and over the next couple of years he watched them improve and develop, but things were moving much slower than he expected.

At one point, Ben created a chart to log each player's weekly practice hours. After a couple of months, it became clear to him that it was simply impossible for them to get in anywhere near enough practice at school. The most dedicated players were training, at most, for five hours a week, and many considerably less. With there being 36 weeks in a school year, that equated to just 180 hours. At that rate, it would take them 55 years to clock up 10,000 hours of table tennis practice. No wonder things were moving slowly!

But it was difficult for them to get in any more hours. They had their academic work to complete. Many of them also played other sports, or instruments, or were in the school drama production. Some of the older ones had part-time jobs. Getting in just five hours of table tennis a week was tough enough.

The 10,000-hour theory was simple to grasp but almost impossible to apply in reality. The average person is just never going to be in a situation where they can perform the massive quantity of weekly training required. What could he do? Were his students destined for mediocrity or to only ever achieve a decent skill level when they hit 70?! There had to be an alternative.

In 2013 Ben stumbled across a different school of thought, one that he was originally introduced to in a TEDx talk by a guy called Josh Kaufman titled 'The First 20 Hours: How to Learn Anything'. "Forget the 10,000-hour rule", Josh said, "What if it's possible to learn any new skill in 20 hours or less?" That initially sounded like nonsense, but after a bit more research it turned out there was more to it than the headline suggested. Josh spoke about the possibility of getting pretty good, very fast - provided you trained every day and engaged in the right kind of deliberate practice.

Tim Ferriss was promoting a similar message in his book The 4-Hour Chef. It promised things like, "It's possible to become world-class in just about anything in six months or less." Again the claim sounded crazy. World-class in six months?! That's almost insulting when compared to the thousands of hours the real world-class performers have put in. But nevertheless the idea that with the correct framework you could get very good at something, very quickly, was exactly what Ben wanted to hear.

It was the combination of these two approaches that led to the formation of The Expert in a Year Challenge. On one hand, Ben wanted to see if anybody (regardless of talent) could become an expert at table tennis provided they did plenty of practice. On the other, he wanted to examine the possibility of rapidly increasing the speed of learning by ramping up the intensity of the training and coaching received.

He began to question everything. Perhaps there was a faster way to learn; a better way. Could he deconstruct the sport and break it down into its most essential chunks? If so, what were they? This process is sometimes referred to as doing an 80/20 analysis; identifying the 20% of work that produces 80% of the results. Not all work is equal and perhaps traditional coaching and training, that tries to create the 'complete player', might not be the only way to achieve success.

Not only did Ben want to get an adult really good, very quickly, he also wanted to shock the table tennis community into taking the challenge seriously. He decided he would publish the progress online and set a crazily high 'expert' target; the top 1% of active participants in a field. With there being roughly 25,000 players registered with Table Tennis England, that led him to aim for a top 250 ranking. To put that into perspective, it took Ben himself about 10 years of recreational play, followed by 9 months of full-time training at Grantham, to reach that level. To do it in a year would be unheard of.

He also wanted the table tennis training to take place around normal life, to show that *anyone* could do it. This meant that shipping someone off to China for 365 days of full-time table tennis was out of the question. The practice would have to take place largely in hour-long one-to-one coaching sessions. 365 days in the year. 365 hours of practice.

It was a long way from the 10,000 hours he had read so much about, but his dissertation had shown him that it takes a typical player roughly 2,000-3,000 hours of practice to get to the top 250 'expert' level. Perhaps 365 hours of this new and improved, high-quality, high-intensity practice would be enough?

All he needed now was a willing participant. Key to his challenge was the idea that talent wouldn't play much of a role, so instead of doing some sort of trials, to identify the best candidate, he decided to simply select anybody that happened to like the idea. At first he was going to see if he could convince Katie, his wife, to do it. But based on her facial expressions the one time she had watched him play, he'd gathered she wasn't much of a table tennis fan. However, Katie did have a good idea and recommended me. Ben asked me the next day. To him, I was the perfect candidate. I had a table tennis table in my flat, didn't live too far away from him, had no background in racket-based sports, and was still very much a beginner.

In my naivety, I leapt at the challenge. This wouldn't be like my rowing, I thought. With Ben coaching me every day I wouldn't be able to skip sessions, and with the progress being recorded online it would be too shameful to quit. Best of all someone who is an expert, not just an expert but a coach, had told me that I would achieve something incredible. By the end of the year, I wouldn't just be better than my housemates, I would be one of the best players in the UK. And all it required was a few hours a week, probably less time than I spent watching Netflix. It was a no-brainer.

Back then I knew almost nothing about table tennis, including what on earth it meant to be in the top 250. Thinking about it now it's hard to believe I knew so little. Spin; one of the most important parts of the game, I didn't even realise existed. Ben, on the other hand, knew exactly what he was proposing. He wanted to train me to a level that hardly any adult starter ever reaches, let alone in just one year. This would be the ultimate table tennis challenge. If we pulled it off it would be a miracle. But despite that his 'Expert in a Year' challenge had so far achieved everything he'd wanted it to. It got me motivated and caused a huge stir in the table tennis community, creating polarising support and condemnation.

The challenge was set, due to commence on 1st January 2014, but before that Ben came round to my flat one Wednesday afternoon to film a 'before' video. The first thing he did was move the table tennis table. We had it squidged sideways in the kitchen section of our kitchen-living room, with less than a metre of space each end. He turned it around so that it went long ways. That meant the sofas were pushed to the side of the room and our lovely, spacious kitchen-living room become solely a table tennis room.

Ben said he wasn't going to give any coaching until January 1st so he just told me which shot he wanted me to hit and then we silently rallied. I remember thinking I'd improved a lot just in that hour, despite him not saying anything. Just rallying with someone who knows what they are doing is a great way to pick up the basics. If you're serious about getting good at table tennis it's really worth trying to get in with a group of players that are at a level above you because you'll subconsciously learn from them and absorb their habits. In hindsight, I can see that my technique was all over the place but at the time I thought I'd done a pretty good job. While we were playing I thought to myself, "I don't want to look too good otherwise people might think I'm already great before starting the challenge". Looking back now, that seems ridiculous.

We had a couple of weeks to enjoy Christmas (and freedom) before The Expert in a Year Challenge began. I was pretty excited to get started and so was Ben. It was going to be one hell of a year. At the end of December, Ben posted a video on YouTube explaining what the challenge was about, here's a clip from it:

"So what is The Expert in a Year Challenge? Well, for the whole of 2014 I have set myself the goal of taking a complete novice, a beginner at table tennis, and turning them into an expert. I have teamed up with a friend of mine, called Sam, and the aim is to try and train him 5-6 times a week, for an hour at a time, for the whole of 2014 and turn him into an 'expert in a year'."

It's almost funny reading that now. Now that I know what is required to get to that level and how much work we actually put in.

3
THE FIRST 31 HOURS

"If the power to do hard work is not a skill, it's the best possible substitute for it." – James A. Garfield

1st – 31st January 2014

As soon as the fireworks were over, just after the bells stopped striking midnight, I made my excuses:

"Sorry guys I've got to head back, I need to get up early tomorrow to play table tennis".

"Umm, what?"

"Yeah, from tomorrow I'm going to be playing table tennis every day for a year, coached by my friend Ben."

Ben's New Year's Eve was even more awkward. Whereas I was just at a house party on the other side of London, he was at a cottage buried deep in the countryside. The rest of the group were staying until the 3rd, but not Ben. On New Year's Day, he woke Katie up early and groggily got her and their stuff into his old, falling apart car. It was an awful journey home, pouring with rain, and every few miles the engine kept cutting out.

Katie was not impressed. Somehow they made it home safely and Ben immediately got changed, grabbed his table tennis stuff, and navigated the three trains it takes to get to my flat; leaving Katie to deal with the unpacking.

Strange looks and bailing on social events were to become a pretty regular occurrence over the next 12 months. I left a lot of parties early, if I went at all. I was always thinking, "Am I going to get enough sleep? What time is Ben coming round? Am I drinking too much? How am I going to tell so-and-so that I can't make it to their birthday because I have table tennis?" And it wasn't any easier for Ben. Most of the time if I was playing, so was he; or he was at least there to watch and coach. Over the year, Ben spent so many hours on those three trains he'd probably qualify as an expert in commuting.

Despite the annoyingness of starting on New Year's Day, we were both really excited. I had convinced myself that the one-to-one training would be so efficient that it would take just a few weeks before I was head and shoulders above my housemates. I'd watched Ben play and thought, "I'll look like that in 12 months time!"

Ben couldn't wait to put his theories to the test and get our progress online. As soon as he got to mine he started setting up the camera - from now on I was going to have to get used to being filmed constantly – and then we started the training. "We need to get rid of all your current bad habits and shots; they're crap and will hold you back", he told me. So we started from scratch, that whole first hour was spent working on just one shot; the forehand drive.

It started with what Ben called 'shadow play'. Basically, I had to stand in front of a mirror and pretend to play the shot over-and-over. No bat and no ball, just the body and arm movements. Ben would say things like, "lean forwards, keep your back slightly curved, bend your knees, twist backwards then forwards". It all looked very natural during Ben's demonstrations, but when I tried it there was nothing fluid or graceful about the motions. To make matters worse, I was feeling very self-conscious. I had never really been filmed before, and this early experience was of me doing a very bad job at twisting back and forth – looking like a malfunctioning robot.

I should point out though that over the year I grew to love shadow play. It really does make sense to master the correct movements and the feeling of your body before worrying about the ball and your shot. If you haven't used shadow play before I'd encourage you to give it a go.

Physically that first session was easy, but mentally I was exhausted. There was so much thinking involved. "Am I doing this right? Am I doing that right? Have I done that funny thing with my wrist again that Ben doesn't like?" After way too long spent editing, the video from session #1 was finally uploaded to YouTube on 9th January. Once it was online the challenge suddenly felt 'real'. My friends, family, and a bunch of random people I'd never met before could see what we were doing. The pressure was on.

That's pretty much how our sessions went throughout January. We stuck to what Ben called the four basic strokes; the forehand drive, backhand drive, backhand push and forehand push. If you are new to table tennis, these are the shots you need to focus on and it is pretty standard to learn these at the beginning. The drives are your attacking shots that have a bit of topspin and the pushes are your defensive shots played with backspin. Getting comfortable with them, and learning how to play them properly, takes time. We did hours of rallying as I slowly got the hang of the correct movements and contact with the ball.

It was all part of the master plan. January would be spent exclusively on the four basic strokes. Then in February and March we would start introducing some of the more advanced shots such as; the loop, the block, the open-up, the flick, and a few different types of push. By the end of April, I would have reached a good enough level of technical proficiency and could begin learning how to use all of my new techniques in matches. So we had four whole months to focus exclusively on the technical fundamentals. That felt like plenty of time.

It was hard and, frankly, boring work, but I stuck with it and we managed to hit the target of 31 hours of training for January. Back then we were really keen on doing exactly 365 hours (one for every day of the year). If we missed any we would make sure to do two sessions on another day. As I improved, Ben would speed up the rally, add in a bit of movement, or have me combine strokes (for example, one forehand followed by one backhand). Each little addition made it a bit more difficult to perform the skill correctly.

I soon got used to the videoing and it turned into quite a motivational asset (I recommend everyone give it a try). Although I felt like I was improving, we were only really able to see it when we watched back the highlights video from the week before. Each time I would cringe at how bad I looked and marvel at the difference just one week had made. It was an exciting time. Not just with the quick improvement but I was also conquering lots of mini-milestones. Each time Ben said, "OK you're good enough at that now, time to move on to a new shot", I felt like I was completing a level in a computer game. I had gone from nothing to something very quickly. This is what Josh Kaufman talks about in his book 'The First 20 Hours'.

"By completing just 20 hours of focused, deliberate practice you'll go from knowing absolutely nothing to performing noticeably well."

And that's exactly what I experienced. Back in 2013, when I was just messing around with my housemates, I knew pretty much zero about table tennis. I would hit the ball however I liked and hope for the best. I had two options; to hit it or to hit it hard. That was it. Now, after 31 hours of practice, I had a small arsenal of different strokes up my sleeve. I could push the ball with backspin or drive it with topspin. I was much better at deciding whether to use my backhand or forehand. I reckon if you'd asked my flatmates, Toby or Dan, they would have agreed that I was now "performing noticeably well". They'd watch me training with Ben from time to time and my technical improvement was obvious.

But observation wasn't enough. There's no point 'looking good' and losing a match, we needed a true test of my skills. So on the last day of January, after much urging from Ben, I challenged Toby to a match. Despite feeling like I had improved loads, I was ridiculously nervous. If I had dedicated all this time, with one-to-one personal coaching, and still lost to Toby, then had it all been for nothing? Would that make me a rubbish human being who could never learn table tennis? I reluctantly set up my GoPro camera in the corner of the room and the match began with some rock-paper-scissors to decide who would serve. I lost the rock-paper-scissors - a bad omen.

The first match was pretty even, albeit evenly bad. We had short rallies with a lot of mistakes on the serve and return of serve by both of us. Toby took the lead quickly, going 2-0 up, and maintained it as we battled to 10-8. It was my serve, which gave me an advantage. I knew I could win those two points, which would bring us level at 10-10. I took a few short breaths and served; served and missed the table – losing the first game 11-8.

That pretty much sums up the whole match. Shaken from the first loss it just got worse. I became tenser and was quickly losing confidence in my new shots. I lost the second game 11-7 and the third one 11-6. What a depressing end to my first month of training. Even after 31 days of practice I still hadn't managed to get a single game off Toby. In fact, the scores would probably have been similar if we had played in December. Ben tried to put a positive spin on it, telling me that we hadn't worked on any match tactics yet and that at this stage it was more important to play correctly than to win. It didn't make me feel any better though, and worse he was still going to put my humiliation on YouTube.

4

A RUDE AWAKENING

"Waiting is painful. Forgetting is painful. But not knowing what to do is the worse kind of suffering." - Paulo Coelho

1st - 18th February 2014

The morning after the match I woke up disenchanted with table tennis. It was an early start because I was headed off for what would be my only proper non-table tennis holiday in 2014. I had ten days of trying to learn to ski and reflecting on the challenge so far.

Despite Ben's throwing a positive light on it, it was clear that he was surprised I had lost. On paper, I was now a lot better than Toby. Even after just a month of practice my shots had improved a huge amount and I looked like a whole new player. I felt better than Toby, but the scores said otherwise. I needed to deal with it, move on, and try to figure out what had let me down.

I returned home to England, bruised from skiing, but glad to be back to table tennis. The break had given me a boost and time to rekindle my excitement. I was eager to get back on the table but before I did, Ben and I sat down to thrash out a few things that were on our minds.

We had both been impressed by my speed of improvement, I picked up the shots very quickly and within a session I would be doing the movements correctly. But there was something missing that was holding me back. There were just some simple things that Ben takes for granted that I was struggling with. My rhythm and timing always seemed to be slightly off, and more worryingly it wasn't improving. Bad timing and anticipation meant I felt like I was always moving late or standing in the wrong position. It's all well and good having an awesome shot, but it's no use if you're nowhere near the ball when you execute it.

One of the reasons I had gravitated towards table tennis in the first place was because I didn't think it required much natural sportiness. That just turned out to be completely untrue. Table tennis still uses plenty of skills that you can develop through generally playing a lot of sport; such as coordination, balance and timing. All the stuff Toby was good at and put down to his goalkeeping experience, and I had always struggled with. I used to think I was pretty average when it came to things like coordination, but Ben quickly put me in my place. He told me (and the entire internet) that he thought I was "unsporty" and "below average".

If you watch some of the early videos that lack of fluidity or flow is really evident with how stiff I look. My muscles were tense and all my movements were very jerky. All beginners struggle with this to some extent, but I think I was worse than most. When you are learning a new motor skill your movements are quite big and clunky at the start and they become more refined and fluid over time. But we never really let that fluidity come. We approached developing technique in a very conscious and analytical way that meant as soon as robot Sam was getting kind of the correct motion, we moved on.

Part of the problem was how rigidly we were sticking to Ben's training plan. As soon as I got the basic movements of a stroke; we'd tick off that shot and say I could now do it. According to the plan, as it was February, we should have been moving on to more advanced shots like the loop and the block, but as my match with Toby had highlighted, I was still lacking fluency with the basic shots. He had a completely different style of play to Ben, so when he hit the ball it would travel with unpredictable speed and spin. If I wasn't given the perfect 'normal' ball, the quality of my shot quickly deteriorated.

Regardless, we decided to move on and start working on my looping and open-ups. They're both very similar shots but played against different balls. A loop is a topspin shot played against a topspin ball, whereas an open-up is a topspin shot played against a backspin ball. It's not that we thought my basic strokes were perfect, we knew they weren't, it was just that it had become apparent that a year simply isn't long enough to master all the various skills of table tennis to an 'expert' level. Even with a ridiculous amount of private one-to-one coaching, it just wasn't going to be enough. With so much left to learn ploughing on felt like our only option.

The foundation we'd laid down in January proved to be a big help in learning the loops. The beauty of learning correct technique right from the beginning was that the loop is just an evolution of the forehand and backhand drives. Shots I had already spent quite a lot of time on. Ben told me that when he had previously coached adults, they often found the loop very difficult to pick up. Their basic drive shot was incorrect so they had to learn the loop completely from scratch.

Progress was similar to what we had experienced in January. I was moving quickly, picking up the basic technique easily but then moving on before I had truly internalised them. I was also starting to pick up lots of bad habits that would haunt me for the rest of the challenge.

One of the worst ones was my tendency to hit the ball with a windscreen wiper motion on the backhand, which added a bit of sidespin to my shots. That doesn't sound too bad, but the result was that I had no power and my aim was awful. Every backhand shot I played drifted to the left.

To try and fix the bad habits we came up with weird, creative exercises. For a while we put towels on the table so that I could only play into certain areas. In one session Ben made me hold a TV remote in my left hand to try and make me aware of what my free hand was doing - I had this habit of lifting it up towards my chin as I played which brought my bodyweight back. In another, I wrapped a skipping rope around my torso in a desperate attempt to keep my elbows in the correct place.

It was all a bit of a mess if I'm honest. We didn't have a clue what to do. Should we keep trying to go through all the shots one by one? How long would that take? What else could we do instead?

It felt like I was doing so many little things wrong that it might take the whole year just to sort out my technique, never mind actually learning how to win matches. We just didn't have the time with our 12-month (now 11-month) deadline. To be honest, we probably should never have started off this way in the first place. Before the challenge, Ben had been inspired by Tim Ferriss, the idea of hacking table tennis and doing an 80-20. That is what I had got excited about. But now we seemed to be taking things slow, spending over a month doing the same strokes and obsessing over tiny technical adjustments. We were training exactly the same as everyone else, and seeing typical, unimpressive results.

This kind of traditional long-term approach is used very successfully in China. They select sporty kids at a young age (5 or 6) and assign them to sports that seem suitable. Most of the top Chinese table tennis players will have started structured practice at this age. They then slowly take them through all the stages of the sport, first mastering the fundamentals and then moving onto more advanced techniques. They start at such a young age that by the time they are teenagers they have clocked up thousands of hours of practice and have been drilled into little table tennis playing machines. Well good for them, but I was twenty years too late for that approach.

It was obvious that we were never going to succeed following the traditional route. We just didn't have time to get me playing 'perfect' table tennis, but there's a reason all the world-class players play their shots in a similar way: that's the most optimal and efficient way to play them. We clearly couldn't just chuck the technique book out the window. What were we going to do? How could we strike a balance?

Ben needed help, so he reached out to experienced coach Steve Brunskill for some ideas. After some back and forth, Steve invited us to come and train at one of the half-term training camps at his club in Middlesbrough so that he could have a look at me. Ben was excited: "You'll get to play over 15 hours of table tennis in just three days. The coach there is brilliant. You'll also get experience playing in a proper environment and against a variety of players and styles." Conveniently, the camp was just the following week, so we signed up for my first excursion out of 'the kitchen'.

5
LEAVING THE KITCHEN

"As you move outside of your comfort zone, what was once the unknown and frightening becomes your new normal." - Robin S Sharma

19th – 21st February 2014

It was the first of many times over the year I had to be out of bed before the sun rose. I left my flat at 6:15 to get the 7 a.m. train from London Kings Cross to Middlesbrough. I had bought Bounce by Matthew Syed to read on the train, but I got through hardly any of it. I was far too distracted. Running through me was a cocktail of conflicting emotions; I was both terrified and excited.

All my training so far had been with Ben, in private, but now I was really getting thrown in at the deep end. Ben had warned me about the sort of people who go on these camps: top juniors and cadets; teenagers who had been playing competitively for many years. Players much younger than me but some of whom would already be at or beyond the top 250 mark we had set for the challenge.

Then there was little old me, less than a couple of months in and I was expected to be training alongside them. For the first time ever I would be taking my turn as the 'controller'. The player responsible for making sure the other gets a good practice, by directing the ball for them. To the uninitiated that might not sound too bad. How hard can it be directing a ball for someone else? Ha...

But on the other hand, I had three full days of pure table tennis ahead. I couldn't help fantasising about how good I'd be by the end of the camp. In three days, I would get in half a month's worth of training. By the end of it I was sure I'd be able to beat Toby.

I generally have this impression that Middlesbrough is struggling. There aren't enough jobs and it doesn't look like it's going to improve anytime soon. However, one thing that appears to be thriving is table tennis. In quite a small area are some of the best table tennis clubs in the country, churning out many of the top players, including England No.1 Paul Drinkhall. Swerve Table Tennis Centre was a new addition, but even among that exalted pedigree we were really impressed. The centre has a great vibe. It's a full-time club with a café, sofas, and a recreational room. There's also a gym, a sports massage room, and lots and lots of table tennis tables. I can't think of an environment that would be more conducive to good quality training.

We arrived to a great welcome from Steve Brunskill and Paul Warters, the two directors, and I was pleasantly surprised to find that I wouldn't be the only beginner. Shock horror, there were even some players who were worse than me. Even so, I stood out like a sore thumb. I was by far the oldest person training. When signing up for the camp I got my first exposure to how hard it is for an adult to learn table tennis. At the bottom of the form was a compulsory section which needed to be signed by a parent or guardian to allow you to leave the camp to get lunch. There was nothing about age on the form; it just assumed that the player signing up was under 18.

It's not that we chose a kids camp, in fact, we specifically chose one that was welcoming of all ages, it's just that it's almost always kids who go on these camps. The camps are then targeted at kids - a vicious circle. I can only imagine what it would have been like if I had gone to the camp on my own, without Ben. I would have been the lonely old weird guy who's rubbish at table tennis. That's not much fun.

The camp started with a seminar on John Wooden's Pyramid of Success, and in particular the two cornerstones; industriousness (hard work) and enthusiasm. Point taken. I may not be as talented or as experienced as the other players, but I was sure that on these two cornerstones I could beat everyone else.

From there it was onto the first proper table tennis session. We were given set drills where we would regularly change partners. One player would do the drill and the other would 'control'. Oh dear... the controlling. It was even worse than expected. Back then my control was questionable at the best of times but throw in a top player, blasting balls at me with varying levels of spin, and I was left without a hope. Thinking back I consider myself lucky I didn't get a punch in the face. It must have been so frustrating for my practice partners. Fortunately, one of Steve's mantras is that everyone helps each other and everyone was once a beginner, but even so it was still rather demoralising.

The days continued in that fashion, they were pretty hardcore. Lectures, followed by table tennis training, followed by physical training, followed by food, and repeat. We started at 9 a.m. and didn't finish until 4 p.m. That might not be a long day for someone sat at a computer screen, but when it is full of exercise and mentally challenging drills, it's tough.

True to our plan to work harder than everyone else we would get up bright and early in the morning. After breakfast, we would waddle into the hall, with stiff legs, for an hour of pre-camp training. To begin with my legs just wouldn't work, I couldn't return anything and our table tennis was laughable, but half an hour later I was back. Ben even gave me a compliment, "When warming up someone might almost mistake you for a table tennis player! As long as they didn't watch anything else." Tough love. After the official day was over I would do another hour or two with Ben, taking advantage of the extra room we had to practice shots we couldn't do in the kitchen.

The camp was awesome. We got in so many hours of training, I improved a huge amount and above all that, it was really enjoyable. At the end of the final day, we settled down with Steve to talk about strategy and how on earth we were going to achieve this top 250 ranking. Despite how impressed he was with my one month progress, he was still very sceptical about our chances:

"Table tennis is the hardest sport in the world", he told us. "It has the smallest court, the smallest ball, the smallest bat, the quickest reaction times, the most spin, and it's the only sport where you play on one surface but stand on another. You have to play so much to develop the skill, coordination and timing, and you have to learn to cope with different styles of opponent."

We needed to find some sort of 80/20 way of conquering table tennis. Just putting in the hours wouldn't be enough. There weren't enough hours in the year. Tim Ferriss, the author who had introduced us to the 80/20 way of thinking, had done a similar challenge. He managed to win the 165lb weight class at the national Chinese Kickboxing championships after just a year of training.

On the surface, this achievement sounded pretty comparable to our challenge, but after delving a bit deeper we quickly learnt that what Ferriss actually did was win by exploiting loopholes in the rules. He would weight cut (dehydrate himself just before the weigh in and then rehydrate before the fight) so that he was actually a lot heavier than his 165lb opponents. It's a practice that is common in boxing, and other western sports, but wasn't done in traditional Chinese Kickboxing. He also didn't actually do any kicking. Instead, he would use his weight advantage to push his opponent out of the ring three times and win by default, exploiting another rule which was wasn't really utilised. Even though he only spent a year training Chinese Kickboxing, Tim was already an accomplished high school wrestler. He had taken a skill he was already quite good at and turned it to his advantage. In effect, he was wrestling kickboxers who didn't know how to wrestle.

But perhaps *we* could find a similar loophole with table tennis. I had this idea that as the serve was under your control, maybe you could use physics to create a perfect unreturnable serve; one that would clip the edge of the table every time making it impossible for your opponent to return. I theorised that there was surely a specific angle that if you threw the ball onto your bat in just such a way would always hit that spot. Ben just laughed at me. Even now after the challenge is over I still think it's a good idea, but at the time I bowed to his wisdom.

Well, maybe that serve wouldn't work, but there was something obvious we could try. If you asked any accomplished player if there was a way to trick your way to a ranking at table tennis, they would almost certainly answer that you should use 'funny rubbers'. If you have never played table tennis before you probably assume that all table tennis bats are the same; obviously a £100 bat is better than a £10 bat but that is as far as it goes. 90% of the time that's true, and most players have very similar bats, but the rules do allow you to use different types of rubbers.

There are anti-spin, short pimples, long pimples, no sponge, and they all have very different characteristics. Play exactly the same shot, but with different rubbers, and you can totally change the effect on the ball; what should be topspin can become backspin or no-spin. It's enough to totally ruin even an experienced player's game.

In November, I was lucky enough to experience this effect first hand at an over 40s tournament. There was a lot of buzz in the hall because one of the players, Martin Gunn, had turned up with something called a 'hardbat' and was beating people with it. Martin was a good player (usually ranked around 250 in England) and had always used a regular bat previously; but the hardbat was working for him, and he eventually won the whole tournament. Changing his bat had given him an advantage.

I asked him if he thought he played better with the hardbat, but he reckoned he actually played worse. He said the reason he won was that nobody had any experience of how to react to the way the ball was coming at them. His opponents knew how they should be playing him, but their instincts were so hardwired they couldn't override them. It was a lack of experience that held them back. We saw Martin again two months later. He was still playing with the hardbat, and still winning plenty of matches, but he was no longer winning everything. People were adapting. Ben lost to him the first time they played, but six weeks later they played again and Ben won.

Sticking some 'funny rubbers' on my bat could have been a workable shortcut strategy. It would have probably made it more difficult for me to develop into a high-level player but it would have given me a chance of getting some surprise wins here and there against people that didn't know how to deal with the bat. There was something about it that didn't feel quite right though. It didn't feel very much like becoming an 'expert'. We wanted to legitimately get good, not shortcut the system.

Steve suggested focusing on the early points in the rally.

"50% of all points are going to involve you serving. It's the only time you have complete control over the ball. It's not reactive, like every other shot, it's a closed skill. That means it should be easier to become really good at it."

One thing we had been worried about was that a lack

of match experience would prevent me from getting very good in a short space of time. Well, a lot can be forgiven with a world-class serve. Steve went as far as to say, half-jokingly, that I should do an hour and a half of service practice for every 30 minutes of table tennis.

The average number of hits per rally, for professional players, is 4.1 - including the serve. So almost 50% of all shots are a serve or a return of serve. We began to come up with strategies for focusing almost exclusively on the first few balls in the rally; the serve, return of serve, and the next few shots. It's not a revolutionary idea, every table tennis coach will tell you how important the first five balls are, but very few beginners target their efforts in this direction.

Even with this strategy, we still had the problem that these shots could literally be anything. We needed to take the concept further. Dramatically, we decided to scrap a lot of the conventional table tennis skills.

When you watch professional table tennis the thing most people remember is how far back from the table the players are. This wouldn't be me. I was going to try and stay as close to the table as possible. My tactic was to end the rally quickly, so every shot I played should be aimed at killing the point. There would be no blocking or 'passive' play allowed. I needed to be more positive. We knew it was a massive gamble, but we had to try something.

My focus was to be on the attacking shots. We were going to turn me into a super aggressive player with a big powerful shot that I could play for a winner. A short point specialist. A power player.

This tied in with what Steve identified as my 'unfair advantage'. The natural abilities I possessed that my competition did not. As I would probably spend most of the year playing kids and old men, my physical size and strength was the difference. Strangely enough, up to that point I hadn't even considered developing my physical attributes, but if I was going to become a power player it made sense to work on improving my explosive speed and strength. The physical side of training is one of Steve's specialties (he's a personal trainer as well as a table tennis coach) so he gave me a load of exercises to try and a programme to follow.

I improved a lot over the camp, but it still wasn't enough. Despite cramming in so many hours, it was clear that doing the occasional training camp wouldn't be enough to master all the skills needed. By the end of the trip, we had done a total 59 hours of table tennis, 16% of the year, and we were a long way off 16% of the way to top 250! From now on we would scrap the 365-hour target and just aim to do as much as possible.

It had been a really valuable discussion and after saying goodbye to the team at Swerve, and enjoying a £1.48 pint at the local pub, we began the long journey back to London feeling like we had a much better idea of how to go about turning me into an expert in a year.

6
BECOMING MA LONG

"We get old too soon and wise too late" - *Benjamin Franklin*

22nd February - 15th April 2014

When we got home we immediately started implementing Steve's suggestions. The first change was the addition of 15 minutes service practice into my daily routine. I would do it before my training session with Ben, or if I didn't, I would do it afterwards. We also added in half an hour of early morning physical training each day. It started well, and if you watch some of the videos from the month following Steve's camp you will see a lot of skipping, agility ladder running, and lots of exhausted panting.

My cardio improved, I learnt to skip, and I got slightly more agile, but I didn't see any positive transition to my table tennis. After all, it wasn't my fitness or lack of strength and power that was holding me back. I was in no danger of 'gassing out' during a match. If anything, it was my balance and coordination that needed work. If we'd done a bit more of that and perhaps some footwork exercises too, that might have been a good use of our time. But it quickly became apparent that physical prowess has very little to do with table tennis ability, at the amateur level at least. Don't believe me? Go to any tournament, look around, and try to guess who the best players are. It's impossible. The 400-pound obese guy and the 12-year-old kid could well be better than the 21-year-old who looks like an athlete. At one tournament, we went to I asked Ben who the best player was.

"Him", he said, pointing. "*Him?!*" The guy he was pointing to looked like a 45-year-old homeless drug addict. He walked with a slow stoop.

Not only was the physical training largely futile but it also wiped me of energy for the technical sessions and caused me to quickly lose what little motivation I had for the more methodical parts of table tennis. A few weeks after getting back from Swerve I started to skip the occasional service practice. Then I started skipping more and more, and by the time two months had passed I was doing hardly any. Which brings me to the main problem with service practice; it is so boring! Seriously, it's rubbish. It's just repetition of the same movement over and over again, and then frustration when you keep messing it up. No wonder most people don't really practice it!

There is a story about David Beckham that is told to explain how he became one of the best footballers in the world. After training sessions, when everyone else had gone home, he would spend hours on his own just practicing his free kicks. Then he'd go home for tea and continue practicing his kick technique on his younger sister's cuddly toys. He couldn't get enough of it. It's borderline obsession. I can just imagine him kicking his entire bag of footballs, and then having to run around the pitch picking them all up just to start again. In my mind, service practice is the table tennis version of practicing free kicks. David Beckham clearly had industriousness and enthusiasm in abundance; unfortunately I didn't.

I guess that is just the way it is. The true experts find a way to love doing the things everyone else hates to do, and it pays off in the long run. Most table tennis players can't be bothered to do 15 minutes of service practice every day. If you can, you have given yourself a huge advantage over all the other lazy players, like me.

Despite my slacking off, my month or two of on-off service practice still had a dramatic effect. My serves improved massively and quite quickly I was able to 'serve off' non-table tennis players with my heavy spin. The proof of this really came when I finally had a rematch against Toby. It was March 21st a little over a month after getting back from Swerve. We had been out for a couple of drinks, when after a bunch of heckling from Ben, and some bravado on all our parts, we agreed to a rematch. As we stepped up to the table, despite the confidence building alcohol in my veins, I was practically quivering with nerves. I really, *really* didn't want to lose and see a repeat of my humiliation.

This was a very different game to the time before. Toby is very good at a flat, little spin game played at quite a fast pace, but with my new serves I was able to totally nullify his skills. I served pretty much solely heavy backspin, a type of spin that he hadn't come across much before. He would either underestimate how much spin was on the ball (and put it in the net) or if he got it back I would just keep digging the ball at him until he messed up. It wasn't glamorous, and it wasn't flashy, but there was never any doubt who was going to win. Ben was really unimpressed.

"I want you to go for your proper power shots. A top player will just walk all over you if you play so passively".

He was referring to how I never bothered attacking, simply keeping heavy backspin on the ball and waiting for Toby to mess up. What a change from the end of January though. We had gone from Toby beating me easily to: 'of course you'll beat Toby if you play safe, but you should be pushing yourself'.

During our actual table tennis sessions, we put a massive emphasis on the 'open-up', a loop that turns a slow backspin ball into a fast topspin one. I had started working on it seriously at Swerve and actually picked up the basic movements very quickly. In one multiball session on the last day of the camp, I was doing these big, powerful forehand and backhand open-ups. After it Ben was beaming:

"If we don't make it, people will look back at this video and wonder how on earth we failed!"

But that initial progress had given us a false sense of where we were at. Our entire approach was pretty ridiculous. We said to ourselves;

"Let's forget about how Ben plays his open ups and just copy the best players in the world. Surely their technique is better."

Ahh, it is so silly thinking back now. We would sit hunched over the laptop watching fuzzy YouTube videos of Ma Long, the world no.1, doing open-ups.

"I think he's doing this with his legs", I would say, as I tried to re-enact it.

"Umm, no. I think he's doing this", Ben would reply.

I doubt either of us were right. We couldn't even see his legs because of the angle of the camera. Despite having never really done an open-up before, I immediately started trying to execute with the same speed and power as the best players in the world. As I said, it was a ridiculous idea.

We continued to work really hard on my power game during March and April, and the quality of my strokes did improve massively. If you took the highlight reel from a bunch of my games against Ben it would look very impressive. I was always going for a kill shot or a powerful open-up, and when I executed them correctly they had good technique and a lot of power. Boom, they would get blasted past him.

Well, they would some of the time - most of the time I would miss. The way we were training meant that I was doing shots that were miles above my 'level'. It was as if

5% of the time I looked like a top 250 player but during the other 95% I looked like a fool. I had no consistency or accuracy. It was a hit-and-hope style of play. And on top of all that, my big powerful shots were very predictable too. I would almost always blast them to one or two of the same places, and because my technique was quite robotic and involved big movements it would be obvious where I was aiming and a simple block from Ben would win him the point.

We realised I still had a lot of technical bits to work on, and that wasn't even our biggest concern. Worse was my shocking ability to transfer my practice level into matches. When doing drills I always looked quite impressive; I was fast, I could anticipate where the ball was going, and my shots were big and powerful. But in matches it would all fall apart, especially if I found myself playing someone other than Ben.

I was desperately in need of more match experience, so in April we signed up to another training camp, this time run by coach Eli Baraty at The Harefield Academy, a school in North West London. It would be two full days of table tennis and, even better; it was close enough that we could commute there each day. No need for expensive trains or hotels.

At the camp, I was able to play against a lot of different junior players, some of whom were pretty good, but most of which were very average. I was expecting to get quite a few wins, but when I played exactly the same shots I did in the kitchen against Ben they kept going off the end or into the net. I couldn't understand it. Ben was much faster and better than anyone I was playing against here, but I actually felt like I had less time with these players. I felt awkward, always in the wrong position and I was constantly misreading the ball. Maybe I just needed a lot more match practice than we had originally thought.

Each time I worked with a new coach I found that they always had their own specialty; a set part of the game they wanted me to focus on. In fact, a few weeks earlier I had done a one-to-one training session with Sherwin Remata, a top 100 ranked player in England, and he had got me to practice my open-up in his particular way, swinging both arms into the shot simultaneously. The session had been brilliant and I learnt a lot, the only problem was that his way of doing open-ups was completely different to Ben and Steve's. Each way was correct; they just had slightly different emphases.

Eli was no different, he too had his favourite coaching tips and luckily they didn't contradict anything Ben, Steve or Sherwin had told me before. He wanted me to improve the deception on my serves and add what he called 'the whip' (a snap of the forearm that added acceleration) to my forehand loop. This was the first time I had heard of 'the whip', but it would haunt me for much of the rest of the year, with me only really mastering it much later on. The service deception, on the other hand, was absolutely brilliant.

I was feeling quite proud of my spinny serves by this point - Eli showed me how far I still had to go. It was too easy to read exactly what spin I was putting on the ball and any half-decent player would be able to find a way to attack my serves with ease. Eli's tactic was to do the same serve, but add in a flurry of arm and wrist movements to try and confuse the opponent. It was something that was so simple, an action that doesn't even involve the ball, but makes your opponent's job so much harder - a great lesson.

The week after, on April 16th, we returned to Swerve. It was an entirely more relaxed journey this time round. I knew what to expect, we were pretty pleased with my progress, and we were both keen to show Steve how far I'd come. There was also a boy called George who I wanted a rematch against. Despite being only ten years old, he had been at a similar level to me on our first trip. I knew that I had massively outworked him over the past two months and wanted to see how I would fare now. After two long days of training, and just before we headed back home, George challenged me to a match.

"Sam looks quite a bit better than George" - Steve commented, as we started warming up.

The match started well. My new serves were giving him a lot of trouble. I grinned slightly as he pushed serve after serve into the net. I won the first set convincingly. I had been very nervous before playing him - what would it mean if I lost? But after that first game I was practically strutting about.

Then something changed. He got used to my serves and instead of pushing them in the net he figured out how to return them. Overly confident, I kept going for these big wild attacks and messing up. Before I knew it he was on the verge of winning the set and it was too late. Despite calming my game down he managed to win the second game. What a mess up. I had been too confident and squandered my lead. The battle continued and eventually, after a hard fought few games, he won the match. I had lost.

How could this be? Even with my powerful loops, much-improved serves, my deception and all the extra hours of training I had put in, he had somehow managed to beat me. George's improvement was more subtle. I'm not sure how to describe it except by saying that he was much smoother than me and just seemed to 'get' table tennis. Whereas I was always late for the ball, he seemed to be there early. What was going on?! Was George proof that Ben was wrong and that the challenge was futile? Can you really only absorb table tennis if you start learning at a very young age?

7

GETTING INTO THE SWING OF
THINGS

*"If you continuously compete with others you become bitter, but if you
continuously compete with yourself you become better." – Unknown*

16th April - 13th July 2014

The long train journey home from Swerve was quite
subdued. Both of us were feeling down and a bit confused.
Is there something about the young developing brain that
means it learns quicker? Is there something about the adult
brain that means it's overloaded and finds it difficult to
react quickly? The thing is, from a logical point of view I
thought I should be improving faster than the kids – most
of the time they're messing around and not watching the
demonstrations, whereas I sit in the front row avidly taking
notes and working through the drills in my head.

There were a few really low points in the year, and this
was one of them. There is something incredibly
demoralizing about losing to a 10-year-old boy. I mean
what else is there in life that a 10-year-old could beat me

at? It was pretty clear that I was improving fast, but my ego was upset that for all the work I was putting in I wasn't improving faster.

I wanted to be George, who seemed to pick everything up immediately. I didn't want to be Sam who needed hours and hours of hand-holding just to get the basics. To be honest, it was a pretty humbling time. I didn't just want to get really good at table tennis, I wanted to naturally be amazing at learning table tennis - a completely illogical emotion and one that I couldn't do anything to improve.

I think if it was just that George was improving quicker than me, it would have been fine. Harder for me to grasp was how it seemed that even though his technique was worse than mine, he would always manage to get to the ball in plenty of time. I, on the other hand, would still be stumbling clumsily as the ball whizzed past. That side of my table tennis just didn't seem to be getting any better. I was just as clumsy when playing George this time round as when I had first played him back in February.

Despite the occasional setback and ego-blow, my training had been going really well - we were clocking up some serious hours and I don't think a week went by without some obvious improvement. My technique was getting sharper and sharper. By the time we got back from that second Swerve camp, I had done 138 hours of training and we were 107 days in.

But it was clear that we were missing something. I needed some of whatever George had. I was more like a robot programmed to do certain huge shots if the perfect scenario presented itself. George was 'reading' the game and adapting himself to whatever situation he encountered. He had figured me out and adjusted. Ben formed a hypothesis:

"So far almost all of your matches have been against me. I'm so much better than you that you need to play really high-risk shots to have any chance of winning points. The way you play against me should be very different to how you play against people at your level.

What you need is a training partner at a similar level to you."

To give me a more even training partner, Ben decided to try playing me left-handed. It was a tactic he had used quite a lot when coaching young kids at school. He was quite good left-handed but nowhere near at his right-hand level.

We played a match and two things quickly became evident.

1. Ben was slightly better than me left-handed, but he was within touching distance. I felt that, with a few more sessions under my belt, I could beat him.

2. I played much worse against Ben's left hand than I did against his right.

Thinking back now I find it hard to believe how much that second point really surprised us. I mean, it should have been obvious and expected. I had only ever really left the safety of my living room for the occasional training camp, meaning that of those 138 hours, a full 110 of them had been playing Ben's right hand. No wonder I looked good against it, I had seen and internalised his game. Likewise, no wonder I was rubbish against anyone but Ben, my experience had been so lopsided. That needed to change.

In May, Ben started taking me along to a local table tennis club. The bulk of our training would still be one-to-one but each week I would also get to practice against lots of different people falling on the full range of skill levels; from total beginners to players at the top 250 level I was aiming for.

The club Ben chose, called ISH, played on a Sunday evening out of a small basement room in the International Students House on Great Portland Street. It was small, with a low ceiling, cheap, and for adults. Yes, that's right, for adults! I had finally found out where all the adults were hiding. So far, at every camp or training session I attended, I had been the oldest person there. Here, finally, was a club with adult beginners and improvers, and boy was it a different atmosphere to what I expected.

On entering the club, I was met by an incredibly diverse array of people. Whenever I mention my table tennis challenge, one of the first (of many) jokes often told is: "You'll be the only non-Chinese person!" Up until now I hadn't really come across any Chinese people playing table tennis, but they were certainly present at ISH. There were retired people who would come in with their walking sticks, young guys taking a few hours off studying at university, well-to-do businessmen in nice suits, and more distinctive characters that would play with their heavy fake gold chains jangling about.

One chatty person, who eagerly welcomed us on that first session, was quick to tell me that the area I lived in, Dalston, was much better in the old days.

"There was this great pub I used to go to. It had free snooker and cheap drinks. There were generally a few fist fights each night over whose turn it was to play, but that was part of the fun. Now everything is too expensive and civilised."

If you say so...

The sessions were much more casual than the coached training I experienced previously. In fact, it was much more like the way I used to play with my housemates before the challenge even began. We'd mindlessly do some rallying and then play matches until we got bored. There was no structured coaching or someone to give you technical tips. You would just partner up with someone, wonder up to the table and hit balls at each other until your time was up and then another pair would take your place. Some of the players were very good, but none of them looked good. I'd look at someone and think, "He can't even play a forehand". He'd be swinging the bat in a horribly inefficient way that looked jerky and clunky. But then we'd step up and play a match, and he'd batter me 11-0.

It was amazing really. These players had been practicing

their own made up technique for years and had got really good at it. The thing is, they would get as good as it's possible to get with such bad technique and then they'd hit a ceiling. No matter how much time they put in they weren't going to get much better. But they couldn't now learn the correct technique because it would mean throwing out the habits of decades and reverting back to being 'rubbish'. It turns out these players go through the same thing every generation. They play 'up-and-coming' kids, beating them easily for years until the kids finally surpass them. Then that's it, they never beat them again. No wonder they think that kids have some natural inherent talent that adults lack!

Don't get me wrong. These adults are trying their hardest to get better; it's just that there are only limited opportunities available for them. One of the local players that I became friends with was Paul. Paul had been playing for quite some time and was much better than me, albeit with some funky technique. Paul was passionate about table tennis and kept inviting us to come and train with him on Friday evenings.

"I've got this great place to train. It's by Kings Cross Station and we can play for as long as we want. Quite a few of the more serious players from here come down each week to practice."

We eventually agreed and one Friday night we headed down. We arrived at about 10 p.m. and waited outside the station because we had no idea where we were going. We weren't sure what to expect and phoned Paul to come and find us. Then, in the distance, we saw him striding towards us. He's about 6 foot 2, and was wearing all of his table tennis gear and a bandana; bat in hand, in the middle of King's Cross Station.

He led us past an outdoor cinema, an area of deck chairs, and a fountain display to Central St Martin's College, an impressive looking university building. Once we walked through the doors we could immediately hear the 'ping' and 'pong' of table tennis balls. We turned the corner and in front of us were four outdoor table tennis tables, inside a stunning reception/lobby area.

This "great training place" was just some outdoor tables in the middle of a student building! There we were, trying to navigate gusts of wind, playing with people in their 40s and 50s, while amused and slightly confused students looked on.

The thing is, Paul was right; this outdoor, public student centre was probably the best place he could train on a Friday night. There just aren't really that many other venues available. Paul told me that he'd tried some of the more established clubs in London but found that a lot of the 'better' players didn't want to practice with him. It's easy for that to become another vicious circle. You decide, as an adult, that you want to get good at table tennis. You go along to a decent club but because you haven't got a clue what you are doing nobody wants to play with you. So you either train with someone else who is just as bad, or you leave and find somewhere more friendly.

How did these good players, who don't want to train with you, ever reach that level in the first place? Well, they were clever enough to start playing as children when they could just turn up to any club and have a coach enthusiastically start teaching them how to play. It sometimes feels like the whole structure of table tennis was set up to make life as difficult as possible for the adult beginner.

The adult beginner's experience of table tennis is generally hitting forehand to forehand and then playing some matches in an overcrowded club once or twice a week, while the child beginner is offered super-systems developed by coaches like Steve Brunskill, honed and developed over years to create the perfect learning environment. It's easy to see why five years in, that child beginner is so much better than the adult.

Our one-to-one sessions were still going well but in June we decided to spice it up. I still needed more match practice so we created a competition. For every session that month I would play Ben in a match where he was left-handed. To raise the stakes, for each set that I won Ben would have to pay me £1, for each that he won I would have to pay him. I predicted that Ben would start off winning most of the games, but that as time went on I would get better and better until I could hold my own. I was confident I would be winning by the end of the month because I was improving so quickly.

The month started and Ben quickly took a strong head start, winning match after match. But I always felt close to him. It was the highlight of each training session. I would pump myself up and I try to psyche Ben out - looking for any perceived weakness to push my advantage. For the first time in the year, I was experiencing the hyper emotions you get when in a competitive match you really care about. There were a couple of disasters where I would work myself up and see red after losing the first game. I wouldn't stop but would go on to lose four or five back to back; continually rechallenging Ben, getting worse each time, and stacking loss on top of loss.

It was a great lesson in match composure and controlling your emotions. In fact, all in all, June was probably the month where I improved the most. The constant competition plus being released into the world of recreational players was really amazing. Although Ben eventually beat me in the competition, it was close and I won my fair share of matches. Not only that; but Ben's left-handed game had improved significantly as well. If he had stayed consistent throughout the month I'm sure I would have been smashing him by the end.

Come July I was starting to regularly win matches at ISH as well. It was quite a strange situation. Because we had our targets set so ridiculously high I was struggling to take pleasure from my victories. I had got to the point where I could really easily beat almost any recreational player - sometimes just by serving them off the table. I was at a level where most people who hadn't played table tennis competitively would think I was really good. But I was still miles off that top 250 goal. Those elite players could beat me just as easily as I beat the beginners. I would focus on the people "I should be beating if I want to get top 250", rather than the people who had been beating me just a month ago and now I was battering.

We passed the halfway point in our journey, but I definitely didn't feel halfway to a top 250 ranking. We needed to step up my training even more. It had been convenient to do all my table tennis with Ben in the comfort of my own kitchen - convenient, but far from optimal. I had no peer group of friends to compete with. I had no players at a level just above me to strive towards. I was lacking the community feel of "being a table tennis player", and the opportunities to share my progress and struggles with others in a similar situation. That was clearly something I needed. The only problem was where to get it. I was attending ISH once a week, but it wasn't really what I was after. What I needed was another Swerve, run by someone like Steve Brunskill, in East London, and ideally aimed at adults.

Unfortunately, those kinds of places just don't exist. There simply aren't clubs that will provide that level of support for the adult beginner. Fortunately, the summer was just around the corner and there were training camps left, right and center.

I signed up to two; the B75 International Training Camp in Denmark and the Eger Table Tennis Camp in Hungary. It was going to be a very busy summer, but I was sure that these training camps would give me access to the kind of optimal training environment that the average adult beginner could only dream of. I was going to outwork all of my competition during the summer and be ready to begin competing at the start of the 2014/15 table tennis season in September.

8
B75, DENMARK

"The difference between an amateur and a professional is in their habits. An amateur has amateur habits. A professional has professional habits." - Steven Pressfield

14th July – 23rd July 2014

If I thought I was nervous going to Swerve for the first time that was nothing compared to how I felt the night before we left for Denmark. Ben first visited the B75 Table Tennis Camp in 2011 and had spent much of the last six months eagerly telling me just how hardcore it was. He delightedly told me how each morning he would have to start warming-up half an hour early just to wear out all the aches and pains from the previous day. How everybody was super keen and would spend their spare time training and warming up. How there were only two English speakers on the entire camp, including him, and everything was in Danish or Chinese. How they told him his technique was completely wrong and he had to relearn everything. How the quality of both the coaches and players was really high.

That is the sort of thing Ben thrives on; hardcore training with players who are much better than him. As he told the stories you could see him shivering with anticipation. I don't think I've ever seen him so excited. But while he thrived on the idea of no one speaking English, it terrified me. He loved the idea of being surrounded by better players. I was stuck worrying about what my controlling would be like. How much astronomically better than me will they be if they told Ben his technique was all wrong?!

Two delayed flights and an hour's drive deep into rural Denmark later, we finally arrived. Although at that time of year Denmark is light for almost 20 hours a day, we had arrived at midnight, it was pitch black and almost everyone was fast asleep. We were welcomed by two hyperactive girls, probably in their late teens. In flawless English, they admonished us for arriving so late and with boundless energy they ushered us to our room.

I'm not entirely sure what I was expecting. I knew it wasn't going to be a 5-star hotel because I had been tasked with bringing a sleeping bag. Perhaps a dormitory or something similar to the youth hostels I used to stay in when holidaying as a student. But whatever it was I was expecting it wasn't a classroom. We were each handed a thin mattress and led round a school to what they described as the "adults' room".

In pitch-black we groped our way into the classroom, careful not to trip over the bundles of human beings curled up all around the floor. At the back of the room I could just about make out a pile of desks that had been pushed to the wall. I found some empty space and, trying my best to be as quiet as possible, rummaged through my suitcase for the sleeping bag. Finally tucked in and with my eyes getting accustomed to the darkness I peered round at my fellow roomies. What would they be like? I had this image of Olympic sized and skilled table tennis fanatics.

This would be my home for the next ten days. Over the sound of harmonious snoring, I finally drifted off to sleep.

God save our gracious Queen
Long live our noble Queen
God save the Queen

After a hurried breakfast and a quick introduction to the other members of the room, who happened to be mostly English people Ben had recommended the camp to, we entered the main hall for the opening ceremony. It was a huge room, filled wall-to-wall with table tennis tables. Lars Rokkjaer, the organiser, introduced each country represented by players. He had every flag and would ask the players to stand up as a snippet of their national anthem was played. Even the mayor of the local town, Sindal, was there. After introducing the players, Lars moved on to the coaches. Oh my word. I was totally gobsmacked at their calibre. There was an ex-world champion and a number of previous and current top 100 world-ranked players, many of whom were now coaching their national teams.

Unfortunately for Ben, the camp had become a lot more international since he was last there. No longer would he have to try and guess what the coaches were saying; now the official language was English. There went one of my biggest fears. The other, that all the players would be unbelievably good, was partly dispelled as well. There were plenty of brilliant players, but there were also quite a few at a similar level to me.

I was put in the second bottom group, Group K. That's right, despite my fears I was only in the second to bottom group! It was headed up by Per Rosin, who is a full-time coach at Kungsängen BTK in Sweden, and Lei Yang, who is a former Chinese National Team player (ie. he was once good enough to be in the top 20 in the world) and is currently the technical coach of the German

National Team. So, in other words, for the next ten days I would be working with Timo Boll's coach. Timo Boll is about as close to a celebrity as you get in table tennis.

As soon as I was introduced to the group my nerves disappeared. Per was very friendly and so were all the players. It felt different to any other camp I had been on as we were all at a similar level and I knew I wouldn't have to train with anyone who was intimidatingly better than me. We started off by playing a few matches. I won some, lost some, and landed around the middle of the group. That had never happened before!

As I got chatting to my new training partners I realised something else. I had got used to being the old guy on these camps, but this time my relative ancientness wasn't too bad. There were a couple of 18-year-olds and another guy in his 20s. Beyond that, I was massively benefiting from the official language being English. Instead of feeling like an outsider in a foreign country, I was the only person completely fluent. Everyone else, including the coaches, had English as their second language. I wasn't the weird old guy who couldn't understand anything (as I had feared I might be); I was more like the cool older kid who everyone looked to, to find out what was going on. It was a very unusual experience and a pleasant surprise.

The training got under way and proved to be pretty hardcore, but in a good way. We had four meals a day and three training sessions. In the breaks, I would hunt down different coaches to try and get some extra tuition. In the back of my mind was something Steve Brunskill had told me on my first trip to Swerve. He said that the best player was the person who did more than anyone else. I tried to cram in as much as possible and would grin to myself when entering the hall during a break to find that I was the only one training. By the end of the first day, I was shattered but happy.

The mornings were really grim. I would slide from my sleeping bag, feeling stiff and cramped. Half the room would still be asleep so I'd quietly put some clothes on and give Ben a prod with my foot, subtly indicating to him that it was time for breakfast. We would stagger out of the school building and over to the training hall where we'd load up on coffee and cereal. Once the coffee got our brains working again it was time to prepare for the morning session. That involved a visit to the communal shower rooms, very hastily done for the fear of a little kid walking in (I fear us English are a bit more prudish than the Danes), and then 30 minutes or so of warming up, stretching and hitting some balls in preparation for the first session.

The days would be spent training, sweating and aching, while the nights involved sleeping on a thin mattress, on the floor, surrounded by snoring men. I knew the week would be tough and I'd be roughing it, but what I didn't realise was how much I'd enjoy it. The days were physically and mentally shattering, but there was something pure about it. While at home I would often get up, play table tennis, do a full day's work, and then play table tennis again. The split focus was exhausting. In Denmark, all I had to think about was table tennis. There was no worrying about work, money, or keeping social engagements. I didn't even need to think about the food I was eating or its nutritional makeup. It was all taken care of.

It was the first time I really got to appreciate the benefits of being a 'professional'. There is something special about having your sport or skill as the sole focus in your life. No wonder professional sports stars reach such peaks of excellence. They're in a perfect storm of focus, training intensity, competition, nutrition and coaching. How could they possibly not get awesome?

This was also my first time realising what a bubble high-level training is. Everyone on the camp was comparing themselves to each other; "How long have you been playing?" was a common question. The purpose of asking was simply to try and work out how good everyone was at similar points in their career. I would strut around telling people I had only been playing for six months but, as I'm sure you're aware, that wasn't the full story. The average beginner doesn't train very much when they first start, whereas I had been playing near enough every single day and had a personal coach.

I learnt a lot from the camp. The coaches generally seemed to be the sort of people who really want to see you improve. Per, in particular, let me hassle him into doing a lot of extra one-to-one training. But it wasn't just the training that was so beneficial - being surrounded by dedicated hard working players, who were also much better than me, was brilliant. I think I probably learnt just as much through some strange sort of osmosis as I did from the direct training. All day, every day, I was surrounded by good quality table tennis. No-one had bad technique and there were very few bad habits for me to pick up. If I could have stayed at that camp for the rest of the year, without it costing me an arm and a leg, I probably would have.

Don't get me wrong, it wasn't all fun and games. I still had to endure my least favourite part of table tennis practice; controlling the ball for my partner's exercise. I had been terrible at it at Swerve and, although I had improved since then, relative to the quality of my training partners I was still very much a novice. I could hold my own in the group in everything, except blocking. There was one particularly traumatic time when I was blocking the ball for Hrefna, an Icelandic girl who had just joined our group. She was doing a drill known as Falkenberg, and over the half an hour we did the exercise I don't think we ever got beyond the third block. Luckily she was polite enough not to throw a tantrum. Ben happened to be watching this exchange and I could see he was trying not to laugh. Afterwards, he told me he was worried that if he said anything I might have flipped out and given up. I was obviously finding it massively frustrating.

Physically the camp was really tough as well. After a few days, my whole body was constantly aching and it wasn't long before the injuries started. Ben badly hurt his back, getting a similar injury to one I'd had a few months earlier, and just in my small group of eight players, five had to sit out at least one session due to injury.

The main take away from the camp was a shift in attitude towards how we managed my training. There was a massive difference between my level of play in practice and during match situations, just like had been pointed out while at Swerve, but we began to put this down to the traditional way I had learnt to play. It's typical to learn via simple drills and then transition to more complex drills and finally match situations, but they are big steps that require a lot of practice. We had a very short time-frame and needed to start improving my match-play as soon as possible.

After discussions with various coaches (and in particular, some good advice from Istvan Moldovan, a world-class Norwegian table tennis player turned sports psychologist) we decided that from now on all of my training would be directly relevant to match-play. For instance, if I wanted to train my backhand open up we would create a drill that involved a point situation including a serve and return. That way there would be some decision making involved, but we could limit the options enough that I could focus most of my attention on improving that one shot.

The training with Lei Yang (my Chinese coach) took a very different form. He didn't speak much English and did most of his coaching via demonstration and multiball. As you can imagine from a 'technical' coach, it was very very technical. He would get me to do a shot as he fed me balls and then shake his head.

"That is bullshit!" he would say as he walked over, adjusted my position and got me to make a slight change to how I hit the ball.

"That is crap".

Slowly I improved, or got closer to what he wanted from me, and eventually I was able to coax what was almost a compliment from him.

"Good. Good."

His advice really showed the way he had been trained and how much of a different level he was on. I once asked him how much service practice I should do.

"Not too much, maybe 90 minutes a day."

He had been brought up playing table tennis practically full-time from a very young age. He told me that every day from the age of six he would start training at 6 a.m. It just goes to show the different routes you can take to arrive at the same destination. Istvan's experience of table tennis had clearly been poles apart from Lei Yang's and yet they were still both international-level players that had transitioned to elite-level coaching, and now found themselves at a training camp in Denmark.

It was also apparent that there isn't always a right or wrong answer to the question of how best to coach a player. Istvan downplayed the supremacy of technique and believed other factors such as anticipation and decision making were most important. Lei Yang disagreed. This difference of opinion between the Chinese and European coaches could cause tension and there was one particular session where Group K came to a standstill while Lei Yang and Per got into a bit of an argument about how best to move from one side of the table to the other.

When I had first arrived the idea of playing table tennis full-time for three weeks was terrifying, but by my last day I was so settled and in the zone I felt sad that it was ending so soon. I was very jealous of the extra training and improvement those who were staying the full three weeks would get. My body didn't agree though. I had so many aches and pains. My iliopsoas muscles (the ones at the top front of your legs, by your hips) were so destroyed I couldn't even raise my legs. While boarding the plane, I had to physically lift them with my hands to get up each step.

9

EGER, HUNGARY

"Much learning does not teach understanding." – Heraclitus

24th July – 16th August 2014

Despite being slightly sad to be home I was glad for the rest, but it didn't last long. Ben was away on holiday but had thought ahead and booked me in for some one-to-one sessions with other coaches in London. When he returned in August I really felt like I had made a big step forward. My game was improving and I was a lot more comfortable in matches and competitive situations.

We only had a week of training together before I was heading off again. This time my destination was Eger, Hungary and the safety wheels were off; I would be going alone. I didn't know anyone there and I had no idea what to expect. That's right, Ben abandoned me.

I made contact with Will Maybanks, an English coach at the club, and he helped organise my stay. This trip would be slightly different because I wasn't going to a one-off training camp. Instead, I was going to a full-time club where people train all year round. In other words, I would be joining some professional table tennis players for their standard training. The club had a program in place where amateur players could come out for a week or two whenever they felt like it. There would be two training sessions a day, each about two and a half hours long, one in the morning and one in the evening. I was told that the afternoon would be set aside for lounging around in jacuzzis and enjoying the lovely Hungarian weather. Doesn't sound too bad eh?

I had actually been to Eger a few years earlier for a holiday. I was younger then but the one thing I remember is the wine. Eger is wine territory. There was this lovely valley with over 50 wine cellars door to door selling some of the best wine I had ever tasted for only £1 or £2 a bottle. It was an amazing trip, but this time I was going with the mindset of an athlete and there would be no drinking (or almost none). Instead, I would train hard and come back a changed player.

But when I arrived I found myself right in the middle of temptation's way. My hotel was slap bang in the center of the wine valley and a bit of journey from the town and club. So for much of the day I was stranded in a valley where almost the only thing to do was drink wine - the wine I had promised myself I wouldn't drink! Somehow I managed not to succumb to temptation, too much.

Each morning I would be picked up by one of the trainers and shepherded to the club. The morning session was pretty much limited to just the residential players, which consisted of some local professionals, myself and a few other people who had come to visit for the week. Some had only recently started to learn table tennis and it was a nice surprise to not be the weakest player there.

One very interesting couple from Malta had, in fact, moved to Eger for three months during the summer with the sole intention of learning to play table tennis from scratch. As total beginners, they had decided to relocate and play table tennis almost full-time, six days a week. That's quite a commitment and one that was obviously really paying off in their rapid improvement. They had basically decided to do a much more hardcore version of The Expert in a Year Challenge. Rather than try and fit the practice around their work, like I did, they had gone all out and were fitting everything else around their desire to improve at table tennis.

There was also a group who had come to visit from the UK, and they were mainly older teenagers. It was a very different vibe to Denmark. They were there as much for the holiday and freedom as the table tennis training. This meant that the week could be as hardcore or casual as I wanted. There was no threat of Lei Yang telling me I was "bullshit" if I missed a session.

Our training consisted of a lot of multiball with the coaches and plenty of regular drills. In many ways, it was kind of the opposite of everything Istvan had told me to do just a few weeks ago. Most of the training was prescribed to us, so I didn't have much input into my drills or exercises. Control was given to the coaches to decide how best I should spend my time. I reckon Lei Yang would have felt a lot more comfortable in Eger. In one of our daily group feedback sessions in Denmark he had told the group, in no uncertain terms, that he thought the job of the player is to be silent and listen to the coach's advice.

There was one part of my game that they really focused on in Hungary - spin. I felt like I was getting pretty good at table tennis by this point, but this spin business was certainly one area where I was found lacking.

"More spin", was the phrase I heard most during the week.

"Slower. More spin. Faster feet."

I didn't get it. What did they mean "more spin"? I felt like I wasn't getting anywhere, but I kept trying. I spent the whole week working on "more spin", constantly trying to hit the ball less hard but with extra spin. It's a difficult thing to do. I eventually worked out that I was supposed to be swinging the bat with just as much force and acceleration, but the power was to be focused on a very fine light brush of the ball. I needed to skim the ball rather than hit through it.

It made sense. Table tennis is a spin game after all – that is what separates it from other racket sports. We should have focused on spin right from the beginning (we both admit that now). We stupidly chose power, thinking it was my unfair advantage, which backfired hard. Spin is just a much more effective tool. Anyone can be lucky and block a power shot, whereas spin is much trickier to deal with. Cranking up the power also increases the chance of making mistakes, whereas spin actually helps you to keep the ball on the table. It seems obvious now - if you want to get good at table tennis, focus on mastering spin.

But I was struggling and I returned home from Eger pretty disheartened. I had spent the whole week being told I needed to get more spin on the ball and I felt like I had failed completely. During my final training session, on my last day at the club, I was still being told I needed more spin, just like they'd said on the very first day.

10
FINDING MY GAME

"He has achieved everything. Jan Ove Waldner; Olympic Champion, World Champion, European Champion, known world-wide as the player with the best feeling and even, the best table tennis player of all time." - Donic Table Tennis

17th August – 31st August 2014

I landed back in the UK at 1 a.m. on Sunday 17th August and finally collapsed into bed at about 3 a.m. I was physically and mentally shattered. The last four weeks had been so intense; lots of travelling and even more of table tennis. Ben, on the other hand, had just got back from a family holiday in Cornwall and was keen to immediately get back into some serious training.

He'd arranged for an old teammate of his called Patrick to meet us at ISH that evening and was excited to see how I would fare against him after all my extra practice. He also wanted to hear about Eger and what I had been working on. Thinking back, I can scarcely believe I had the energy to go, but I kept my mouth shut and hauled my aching body to Great Portland Street for an evening of yet more table tennis.

Apart from a few texts telling him about some of the more amusing points of the trip, I hadn't really told Ben anything about Eger. Then as we began warming up, practicing my shots, he commented:

"Wow, you're getting so much more spin now!"

I guess that just goes to show that when you've got your head down training hard it can be really difficult to see your own improvement, even when it's there in abundance. It was nice to hear and I knew Ben wasn't just saying it to cheer me up because; 1, he had no idea I was feeling rubbish about not being able to generate spin; and 2, he never says anything just to cheer me up.

Spin is an aspect of table tennis that is linked closely to something called 'feeling'. "You need more spin, you need better feeling", people constantly said to me. Feeling. I haven't spoken about it at all so far in this book; despite it being probably the most used word in table tennis. Why haven't I spoken about it? Because for the first eight months of the challenge I considered 'feeling' to be the most annoying term in table tennis. As far as I was concerned 'feeling' was some mythical invention that table tennis players had come up with to make us novices feel like idiots. People were constantly either telling me it was really important, or pointing out that I didn't have any. Sometimes it would be both. What on earth does it mean? I may have been starting to get better spin, but my 'feeling' was still awful.

I know one player; let's call him Fred to save embarrassment. Fred has been playing table tennis for years, and not just recreationally, but training hard. He plays 4-6 times a week and coaches younger players. He goes on training camps to help him improve and plays in tournaments around the country. But despite that Fred has never won a game against a ranked player; that is a player in the top 1,000 in England. Why not? If you watch Fred play he has very good spin and some absolutely blinding shots that he can blast past even top players. No matter who he plays against he wins some awesome points. But that is only part of the story, the rest of the time he spends doing massive shots and missing. Fred is a highlight reel player - just like me. He has no feeling.

I was getting very good at massive shots, but controlling the ball in a consistent manner, regardless of what spin was on it, was still a huge weakness. I was determined to change. I didn't want to end up as the sort of player who makes a few wonder shots but spends the rest of the match hitting everything long or into the net. My time in Eger had taught me that spin was key, and there appeared to be a close link between 'spin being your friend' and having the elusive 'feeling'. At this point spin was certainly not my friend, it was an enemy (or perhaps it was more like an annoying older brother that picks on you). Ben, on the other hand, appeared to have this magic 'feeling', it was baffling.

"How did you know what spin that was?" I'd ask Ben after he killed my serve past me.

"I don't know. I didn't think about it. I just hit the ball." He'd reply.

Well, that wasn't much help! There were hundreds of different types and degrees of spin that could be put on the ball by various strokes and serves. Some made the ball swing to the right, others to the left. Topspin could make the ball bounce up, but the downward rotation could also make it drop short. Heavy spin serves make the ball ping off your bat in whatever direction the spin decides. Perhaps all I needed to do was make a mental list of all the different ways the ball could spin and then work out where to stand for each and how best to hit them. Simple – or so it sounds.

For the next week, a typical drill would involve Ben doing a serve and me shouting out which way the ball was spinning.

"In!" I would shout. "Out!"

At the same time, I would have to move into the correct position and then play my shot. I would be watching which way his hand moved during contact and thinking about what that meant for how the ball would curve in the air, and which way the ball would go off my bat. It was mentally draining. During the drill, my technique would be all but forgotten as my focus was on positioning myself correctly and directing the ball.

The idea had some merit, but we took it way too far. I wanted to work out the perfect shot for every particular spin, but that made things far too complicated. The possible variations quickly multiplied and I went from having to learn six or seven different shots to hundreds. I had one loop if the ball was heavy backspin with light left directional sidespin, another loop if it was light backspin with heavy left direction sidespin, and a totally different loop if it was topspin. It was a mess of different spins.

In my head, it made sense but in reality it was impossible to learn like this. After all, if I didn't have time to completely master seven different shots, how on earth could I have the time to master hundreds? What could I do? I needed a different approach.

During that time, I was watching short clips of table tennis most days due to some sort of half-formed idea that watching good players would make me better. One night I stumbled across a video that set off a light bulb moment. It was called 'The Perfect Forehand Loop' by online table tennis coach Brian Pace. I had purchased some of his videos before but at the time they had been a bit too advanced for me so I wasn't expecting much despite the title.

"Without a doubt the forehand loop is the most prominent shot in the sport of table tennis. That is because it can be used in every possible way. You can loop a block, a push, a serve, a chop, a high ball, as well as looping another loop. This makes the forehand loop a trump card because it can come over the top of any other shot played."

Wait a second. Is he saying what it sounds like? That there is one shot that you can do regardless of what the other person has done? Regardless of what spin is on the ball? How is that possible?

The video goes on and Brian demonstrates the mechanics of the shot, the angle your body needs to be at. How you should swing at a 45-degree angle and hit the ball with 75% friction and 25% power. It's the exact same mechanics for each and every shot. Brian isn't a slave to the spin on the ball; he's not worrying about having to work out exactly what is going on before he can react. He is just doing his shot. His forehand loop. His 'trump card'.

I was so confused. How can he possibly do the same shot against a chop (a heavy backspin shot) and a loop (a heavy topspin shot)? It just didn't make sense. If I tried to do that it would be a disaster. I watched and rewatched that video, trying to work out what was going on. Then it struck me. He was hitting the ball at such speed that it didn't matter what the ball wanted to do. The paltry spin already on it didn't stand a chance against Brian's flawlessly executed forehand loops. At the next training session, I was excited.

"I've got it! Feeling is totally the wrong word. It's the opposite of what we want. Feeling implies minute adjustments to convince the ball to do something. That's totally wrong! We don't want to seduce the ball; we want to tell the ball what to do. We want to bully the ball!"

And that become my motto. Under my breath during matches I would whisper, "Come on Sam. Bully the ball." During training I would focus on my technique (the 45-degree angle and 75% friction), just trying to get as fast an accelerated whip of the arm as possible so that the bat was moving at the fastest possible speed as it brushed the ball. I was purely focused on contacting the ball well. If it didn't go where I wanted I blamed the miss on bad timing or a poor contact. No more minute adjustments.

I think throughout the whole year that was the one

change that actually made an immediate and noticeable difference. Overnight a lot of the hesitation and uncertainty was gone. A couple of days later I played someone who just a week earlier was a lot better than me, and I beat him. Actually, I didn't just beat him - I outclassed him.

Ben was less impressed. "What's the difference between what you're doing now and what we were doing when we were trying to copy Ma Long?" he would ask.

"I think your improvement is just because you feel more confident in your shots. You're wimping out of shots less and you don't hesitate as much."

He was kind of right. The Brian Pace forehand was too simple. It had been helpful for sure, but it hadn't taught me 'feeling'. It's also worth pointing out that I'm pretty sure Brian has great feeling and would have been making loads of little adjustments with his forehand loop depending on the situation, it's just that he has been playing for so long it has become so instinctual he doesn't even realise it. On the other hand analysing every possible spin outcome in order to make an infinite number of adjustments is way too complex and would never work in a match situation. So, after all that, I had ended up back where I had started - still not quite sure what feeling was or how best to acquire it.

Then it struck me. I bet if I asked Ben what direction an anti-clockwise corkscrew spinning ball would bounce when it hits the table it would take him quite a while to come up with an answer. However, if I did an anti-clockwise corkscrew spinning serve, without the slightest hesitation I'm sure he would adjust his position so that the ball bounced straight into the path of his oncoming shot. It was this realisation that finally led me to the answer of all my feeling problems.

This principle applies to all sorts of motor skills. Think about walking. Would you be able to describe the process of balancing, leaning slightly forwards, and transferring weight from one foot to the other to enable forward motion without falling over? I couldn't. If you ever watch a robot trying to walk you'll realise just how difficult it is. Even with some of the world's greatest minds they can't explain well enough the mechanics of walking to get a robot to walk anywhere near as gracefully as a five-year-old child. But how did that five-year-old child learn to walk? No-one sat him down and explained the mechanics of walking. He learnt it through observation, experimentation and randomness.

If you ever watch kids at a tournament, what do they spend most of their free time doing? They're always messing around, doing silly shots behind their backs, lobbing the balls up high; all sorts of nonsense that has no part in their real game. I'd always viewed this as a weakness and believed my ability to stick rigidly to the plan was a strength, but I started to wonder if all this 'messing around' is part of how kids learn.

When messing around you see an incredible range of different spins and balls. There is a huge amount of randomness and you try out a lot of different things. You get to experience what weird unorthodox shots do to the ball. It's pretty much the opposite of my hyper specialist training, where I was only seeing a tiny subset of what could happen. Learning through play, as it is often called, is much more likely to create a natural and relaxed looking player. I had become an unnatural and tense looking player. Perhaps this was the key.

We began to think about how we could get this randomness and experimentation into my training without sacrificing technique. We didn't want to spend all our time messing around, but we wanted to add this element somehow.

We tried quite a few things, but one of the best was a drill I called the switching drill. We would start with a normal rally, and then one of us would switch the spin. So, if it was a topspin rally you would have to do a chop and if it was a backspin rally you would have to do an open-up. The rally would continue, with either of us being allowed to switch the spin at any point, and the ball would get weirder and weirder. There was loads of time to experiment and practice and I was still improving my key shot, the topspin open-up.

It helped a lot. I was starting to understand spin and I could feel myself learning quicker again. I had finally started to get this whole feeling business and develop my own game and style.

11

BURNOUT

"That's the thing: You don't understand burnout unless you've been burned out. And it's something you can't even explain. It's just doing something you have absolutely no passion for." - Elena Delle Donne

1st September – 16th September 2014

All the 'messing around' had another big advantage too; my training sessions became a lot more enjoyable. By this point, I was started to feel pretty stressed by the whole challenge. Ranking tournaments were on the horizon and I still didn't feel ready. This new type of training was a lot less intense and I could feel myself relaxing because I was having fun.

We decided to build on that and continued to experiment. We both did some phishing and lobbing (play further back from the table). We also did a load of different sidespin shots and I learnt how to hook and fade the ball. I had a go at the chop-block and a few other wacky shots too. We added in some slower play so that I could get used to controlling the ball in longer rallies.

Basically all of the shots that we threw out back in February and March because we thought they were a waste a time were back on the table. Aghhh, it was so stupid of us! While I might not spend too much time chop-blocking or lobbing in a match that doesn't mean practicing them can't provide other benefits to my game. We had learnt that lesson the hard way.

Ben also started playing as different types of player. He'd create alter egos for me to play against (Glen Larcombe, Ken Larcombe etc.). Some of them would play with funny rubbers, and others would have really peculiar styles. Glen Larcombe, who had a massive pillow for a belly, would only play backhands and had a bad back. He would also cheat. Occasionally Ben would play against me using a placemat or some other random item he found lying around the flat. It sounds stupid but each time I had to work out the best way to play him and make adjustments to my shot.

These sessions were a pleasant break after such a hardcore time away on training camps during the summer. I had come back drained and the mental exercise of trying to classify and turn table tennis into an equation had just made it worse. I often felt like I didn't have the brainpower required to focus during our sessions and was just going through the motions.

At that point, I had another 21 weeks to go and in my mind it had turned into a countdown; "Just a few more months and then you can quit." Before the camps I was thinking, "Oh no, I only have x number of weeks left!" and now I was just wishing for it to be over. It was a complete mental flip that just kind of crept up on me.

I think the technical term for what I was going through is burnout. I'd had enough. I wasn't enjoying it anymore. I didn't really care about the challenge or seeing it through. At least that's how I felt on some days. It was probably the lowest point of the whole year and I was getting increasingly frustrated and irritable during our practice sessions. I just felt angry and annoyed all the time and a couple of mistakes were enough to push me over the edge. Once I 'lost it' it was difficult to get it back and the training would become next to useless. That only further wound me up. During one session, I simply put my bat down halfway through a drill and walked out onto the balcony. I was going nuts and developing this hostile and aggressive personality that I didn't even realise was inside me.

It's surprising the intense levels of emotion table tennis can bring out in you. You think it's just a game, but then I've seen people shouting and swearing, getting into heated arguments, chucking their bat and watching it smash into pieces. There is something about table tennis that can make you go insane if you let it.

These new 'fun' sessions were helping, but it wasn't enough. The sheer quantity of table tennis I was doing was too much and my improvement had stuttered. One day we went on a trip to visit Fusion Table Tennis Club. It was on the other side of London and the trip, which contained just 90 minutes of table tennis, took up most of the day. It was the last straw. On the walk back I finally started letting out all of my feelings to Ben.

"I'm hating this at the moment. I've lost all interest in table tennis and I just want it to be over. I'm sorry, but I need a break. I need some time to relax and regenerate."

I had been afraid to tell Ben. He was just as committed to the challenge as I had been and he had just as much on the line as I did, if not more. I felt that by telling him I needed a break I was really letting him down. I was still a long way off the target we had set, there was only about a third of the year left, and I was asking to take a week off. How could we afford that?

It turned out that Ben had noticed. In fact, he'd been tiptoeing around my temper, not wanting to suggest certain training ideas and feeling nervous about criticising me. He explained that he had been at a loss for what to do in some of our sessions. If I was a kid, he would have told me that my behaviour was unacceptable and given me a good telling off. But as I'm an adult, a peer, and a friend he felt he couldn't do that. He didn't know exactly what was wrong, but when I explained how I had been feeling it made total sense.

"I think that's a great idea. If you take a break now that gives us three and a half months to turn you into a winning machine when you return. It's much better to take the time now than in the middle of tournament season."

So much of success comes down to not quitting; simply continuing to practice and improve over the long-term. I understand now how easy it can be to make rash decisions and decide to quit it all just because you feel really lousy in one particular moment. That's why breaks are so important. You need to make sure you never get to that point where you've had enough and want to throw in the towel.

On Monday 8th September I ran away to the Cotswolds for a quiet holiday where I was determined to not think about table tennis at all for a whole week. The first few days I slept 12 hours a day and did absolutely nothing. It was glorious.

12

TIME TO THINK TACTICS

"By failing to prepare, you are preparing to fail." - Benjamin Franklin

17th September – 1st November 2014

By the end of my week off, I was a changed person. Not only was I rested and feeling more positive, but I was also gagging to get back to table tennis. It was a complete transformation. I couldn't wait to restart training, and I had loads of great ideas and things I wanted to work on.

Originally the plan had been for me to start entering tournaments at the start of the season in September but it was clear to both of us that I wasn't ready. As such we pushed the date back to November, giving me another couple of months to develop some winning ways. We decided that it would be worth going to watch one of the early tournaments anyway, to get a real taste of what competitive table tennis was like at a national level. One of the first tournaments was the Medway Grand Prix and Ben wanted us to pretend I had entered and get the full experience. That meant arriving there at 8 a.m. to get a 45-minute warm-up before the first event began. We would then spend the rest of the morning watching the action.

Just like everyone else who has never been to one, I had no idea what to expect from a 'Table Tennis Grand Prix'. Whenever I asked Ben he would kind of shrug his shoulders and say he didn't really know how to explain it, that it was a hall full of table tennis players and tables. I once asked Katie, Ben's wife, and she told me she had only been once and it was the worst experience ever. They had to get up really early, Ben was stressed out, and then when they finally got there she had to sit on her own all day and had no idea what was going on. Then Ben lost all his matches and they had a really grumpy journey home.

I have to admit that after watching the matches in Band 6 (the entry level group I would be playing in) I felt relieved. The standard was much lower than I had experienced in Denmark or Hungary and I could see plenty of beatable players.

I had my first tournament in less than two months time and I was determined to work as hard as possible to ensure I got some wins and a ranking. We had both realised by this point that I was very unlikely to actually beat anyone in the top 250, but we knew there were ranked players out there that I could beat, especially with another couple of months of practice and experience. It was crunch time and we began analysing the different aspects of my competitive game; physical, technical, tactical and mental.

Despite my lack of any structured strength or fitness training, we both felt that physically I was in pretty good shape. My physical conditioning certainly wasn't going to prevent me from playing well and getting some results. The table tennis alone had kept me in remarkably good nick and I felt much fitter, healthier and a little bit slimmer than I had been back in 2013.

My technique was pretty good too, at least relative to other players at my level. That wasn't surprising - what else would you expect from seven one-to-one training sessions a week? Often I would challenge someone to a match at one of the clubs and after a 10 minute warm up they would look rather sheepish and mutter something about not having a chance against me. After a few points though they'd realise that we were actually pretty 50/50 or perhaps they even had a slight advantage. My technical skill in the warm up would convince them I was a much better player than I actually was. It was time to leave the technical training behind. From now on I was all about the win. Just like Istvan had told me in Denmark; everything should be match relevant. From now on my favourite question would be, "How is this going to help me win more matches?"

That left us with the tactical and mental side of my game. Throughout most of the year, Ben had been telling me not to worry about missing my shots. He said it's better to think strategically than tactically - long-term instead of short-term. This meant making the correct decisions, attacking when I saw an opportunity, and actively trying to make my opponent miss. It was a higher risk strategy but more beneficial in the long run. I like the idea, in theory, because it reminds me of the quote, "Tactics is winning the battle; strategy is winning the war."

But to win the war, I would have to win some battles. If I kept missing, I would lose. I was starting to feel like I might be better off just keeping the ball on the table. It was really frustrating. I felt like even after all this practice I could still end up losing to my little sister (who has no interest in table tennis) if I played in a uber aggressive, hit-and-hope style. I didn't really have a plan B to fall back on. If I wasn't going for my attacking shots I ended up playing what we began calling 'pansy' table tennis. If you want to watch some 'pansy' table tennis in action, check out the final point of my match against Steve Hirst at the Sussex Satellite Grand Prix on YouTube. The point lasted over 20 seconds because we were both passively pushing and tapping the ball over the net, terrified of missing and hoping the other one would screw up before we did. Watching it back now makes me cringe (although I imagine it's much worse for Steve, who also happened to lose).

I felt like I needed to develop a plan B, a conservative but still strong game. I thought that I should be able to dynamically evaluate my opponent and decide which game to play. The only problem was that Ben disagreed. He kept saying I'd get the hang of it in the end and it would all start to come together once I had a bit more experience. He wanted me to "keep looking to attack", as he would say. I had only a few months left, and 'in the end' or 'eventually' might not be soon enough. We either needed to create a whole new plan B or get my aggressive, attacking table tennis more consistent.

We decided that the best way to get my aggressive play more consistent was to utilise 'set pieces' or 'plays'; certain tactics that I could use to predictably win points. These were all based around serving and receiving. I would have certain serves that I could do to encourage my opponent to return the ball in a particular way. Then I would be ready for it and in a good position to win the point. Set pieces suited me perfectly as they sidestepped a lot of the issues I was having with feeling. I didn't need to have great feeling and reading of the ball if I knew exactly what the ball was going to do before the point even began.

Ben got me to read "Table Tennis Tactics for Thinkers" by US coach Larry Hodges. Perfect, I thought. I'm a thinker! Everything made sense to me, but just like every other part of table tennis, it seemed to be much more complicated than I had originally assumed.

One day when Ben's friend Mark Simpson, a top 20 UK player who was playing professionally in Germany, was visiting we decided to work on set pieces. Ben would leave the room and then I would discuss with Mark the upcoming point:

"OK, I'm going to do a short backspin serve to his forehand side and I'm expecting him to do a long dig across court."

"Ok, and what will you do then?"

"Umm, well then I'll be ready to do a big open-up"

"Where will you aim the open-up?"

"Ummmmm, down the line"

"Why?"

"Well, because that gives him the furthest distance to move in order to return the shot"

"OK, good, and what will he do then?"

"Ummmmmmmmmmmm, well because he has hardly anytime he'll probably just block it straight back to me"

"And how will you respond?"

"I'll kill it crosscourt"

"Why crosscourt?"

"Because he has his block in place on the backhand side, it would defeat the point of the kill shot to put it right to where he's already blocking"

It was the perfect plan. Then Ben would come back in, I'd serve short, and he'd flick the ball down the line. Point over. Sometimes the point would work out how I predicted and I'd finish it in spectacular fashion, but the problem was that each step further down the point you go the more possible options there are.

"You just need to keep going until you have every possible set piece hardwired", said Mark.

As I said, it's pretty complicated and took up quite a bit of our time but I ended up with a couple of 'tricks' that I could always fall back on. Perhaps my favourite started with a fast sidespin serve. The sidespin would mean that their return was always dragged to my forehand which meant I could finish it strongly with a loop.

13
TRAIN SMART, PLAY SMART

"I am a big believer in visualization. I run through my races mentally so that I feel even more prepared." - Allyson Felix

2nd November – 14th November 2014

After Mark left he offered to do one-to-one Skype sessions with me every few weeks to help my mental game. A lot of the stuff was pretty straightforward but that doesn't mean they weren't really helpful. It reminded me of something that Steve Brunskill had said to us back at Swerve in February. He was going through this long list of all the things that professional table tennis players do; they practice every day, they make sure they have the best equipment, they give 100% in every training session, they prepare fully for tournaments by arriving early and warming up properly, they work with support staff like sport psychologists, masseurs and fitness coaches.

He said just because you're not currently playing at a professional level yourself doesn't mean you shouldn't do all that stuff. They don't do all of those things simply because they are professionals, they are professionals because they do all those things, and have been doing so for many years. That really struck a chord with me. If you want to be a professional you need to start acting like one.

That all made sense, but then Mark started on something that sounded a bit too much like new age nonsense - visualization; or imagining your way to success. Mark explained that if you imagined yourself training, basically meditated and pretended in your head that you were doing the training, then you would get much the same effect as if you were actually training. He told me about an experiment with weightlifters. The group was split in two, half would lift weights, and the other half would just imagine they were lifting weights. Unsurprisingly the group lifting weights got much stronger but remarkably, the group who didn't do any weightlifting at all, also got stronger. They increased their muscle strength by 13.5% vs 30% from the group actually weightlifting. Wow.

Thinking about my trip to Denmark, I could kind of see what he meant. Throughout that trip, I think that a lot of my improvement was simply from being around so much quality table tennis for so long. The beauty of this sort of visualization is that you can train when you're not physically able to; for instance while on the train during a daily commute, or in the car on the way to a tournament. The problem is that it's pretty tough to keep motivated to do it. If I couldn't keep up with my service practice what chance was there that I'd have the patience to sit still, with my eyes closed for an hour, imagining doing table tennis training. Mark came up with a great alternative though; video.

I'd been using video with Ben since the start of the challenge. Once a week Ben would make a highlights video and we would sit down together and do the commentary before it was uploaded to YouTube. We'd point out all of the things I was doing wrong and what we wanted to work on next week. It was great for helping Ben to plan my practice, but it made me feel a bit useless and overwhelmed. Ben always had a huge list of things he wanted to work on at some point (if there was time) and I had got into the habit of focusing on all the things I was doing wrong whenever I watched myself play.

Unsurprisingly, that was the equivalent of dragging my self-confidence through the mud every week. Mark wanted me to do the opposite, to make a confidence boosting video using some of my best competitive points and set to an inspirational song. It would be a ridiculously cheesy motivational video - my version of the rocky montage.

When it was done it was as cringeworthy as I expected. Three minutes of me winning points against a few different players I'd faced at ISH and Highbury TTC set to a backdrop of Numb by Jay Z and Linkin Park. I knew it was my best three minutes from about half an hour of footage, and I knew it wasn't an accurate representation of how those matches had actually played out, but it still gave me a mini confidence boost every time I watched it. And I watched it a lot.

Another thing Mark suggested was that I spend a lot of time monitoring my arousal levels. Err what?! It turns out arousal in sports psychology just refers to the balance between being pumped up and being calm or relaxed. There isn't a one-size-fits-all approach. Some people play better when they are more pumped-up, others when they are more relaxed. Firstly, I needed to work out whether I preferred to get pumped up or stay calm. Then Mark was going to give me some techniques for altering my state, so that if I realised I was too pumped I could find a way to relax, and vice versa. I think I was best somewhere in between the two.

When I was relaxed I felt calm in my head and could loosen up in my body. The only problem was that any sense of urgency would go out the window and I'd saunter around the court. When I was pumped I would be moving fast and being explosive but my touch and feeling disappeared altogether and I'd often get very worked up mentally until I felt like I was about to burst. From what I've heard from other players this is a common experience and just one of the many things you need to learn to deal with if you are to have any success as a table tennis player. This was never a problem when I was rowing. Rowers want to be as pumped up as possible because it's all about power, speed and pushing through the pain barrier. Table tennis, on the other hand, is an annoyingly fiddly sport.

The final thing I spoke to Mark about was preparing for anything that could go wrong, or something that could throw me off my game. He wanted me to think of strategies to deal with them. To learn to control the controllables as best I could and not worry about everything else. I wrote a list of every single thing that could potentially go wrong and then what I would do if it were to happen. Things like; I forget my bat, so I have to borrow Ben's. And perhaps my biggest gripe - a slippery floor. I hate a slippery floor. It was probably the thing I whinged about the most during the year. Even in my flat the floor was often slippery and it would drive me nuts. A slippery floor might not sound too bad but when you are trying to move quickly and execute powerful shots you really need a good grip with the ground. I had an expensive pair of table tennis shoes, but they still weren't helping me. By preparing for it beforehand, I should be able to control my emotions and not get thrown off.

On 1st November I received a message from Ben, "Fancy playing in a table tennis tournament next Saturday?" My first tournament was scheduled in for Saturday 15th November (two weeks away); it was the Bristol Grand Prix. Ben may have asked, but in reality it was the sort of question you both know isn't a question. I wasn't allowed to say no. I agreed to take part in this last minute addition to my tournament calendar and entered online. Fortunately, it was an afternoon event and we didn't need to get there until 12:30. Most of the others I'd entered had horrific start times, like 8:45 a.m., which meant arriving at 8 a.m. in order to get in that so important warm-up that Ben always bangs on about.

Ben picked me up at about 11:00 and we began the drive down to Horsham. He kept telling me how brilliant it was that this had come up exactly one week before my first tournament. I was just trying to get in the zone. I sat there with my iPad on my knees and headphones in my ears watching my new confidence highlights video over and over. "I've become so numb!" Linkin Park would shout at me. I was already feeling pumped. Nervous, but pumped.

When we arrived we found a table and started warming up next to a load of kids. The place was packed and the other tables were mental with way too many kids trying to play. Fortunately, nobody bothered us at all. I assume, to a 10-year-old, we looked pretty intimidating so we managed to get a good twenty minutes of practice without interruption. Finally an advantage to being the only adult beginner! I needed it too. I felt really nervous. Even just warming up I was missing basic drives and feeling a bit jittery. Every time I missed a shot it felt a bit worse and Ben would look at me like he thought I was joking around. I wasn't, that's just what nerves do to you.

At 1:30 p.m. the tournament started. I'd been put into Band A (the top band) and would be up against the best players at the tournament. I was happy to see that they were all adults or older teenagers because I didn't really fancy playing a bunch of brilliant primary school kids. I was on first against a junior named Jason Morley. I didn't get off to the best start. Point one began with me doing a backspin serve, we both did some pushes and then I opened-up the ball into the net; 0-1. Point two was exactly the same, another open-up straight into the net; 0-2. Point three saw Jason do a fast serve into my backhand, I played a topspin but it clipped the net and went long; 0-3. I glanced over to Ben and saw him looking a bit worried. I could imagine what he was thinking, "Oh crap, he's lost the first three points. Sam, please don't fall apart."

But I didn't. I had a game plan. I had planned to spend the first few shots of the match getting my feel and shots in. I wanted to be doing the high-risk stuff early on, so that I could get used to the conditions and find the best level to play at. The last thing I wanted to do was to get through the first couple of sets and not have done a single attacking shot! I'd be way too nervous to start doing them at a later point. I clawed back some points, settling into my rhythm and finished that first set 8-11 - a loss, but only just. The sets and matches continued. I was losing, but not by much. It was close. I didn't play anyone who I wasn't within touching distance of and I had a great game against a long-pimples player. We left quite pleased with how I had played. I had lost, but I had played well. As I packed away my bat, Ben remarked that he couldn't really have asked for more.

On the other hand Rory Scott, the tournament organiser, had made a point of telling us that everyone I'd lost to wasn't even playing in the top division of their local league. Basically, he was saying, "These players are a long long way from being in the top 250 and you still lost to them all". It was harsh, but true. We knew that from here on the competition was only going to get tougher. The players I'd be up against on the Table Tennis England Grand Prix Circuit were going to be much stronger than the guys I'd played here. It was on the long drive home that it really dawned on us just how tough the next couple of months were going to be.

14

MY FIRST RANKING TOURNAMENT

"If winning isn't everything, why do they keep score?" - Vince Lombardi

15th November 2014

When I started The Expert in a Year Challenge I had this image in my mind of what it would be like. I would get up each day, early, at a time when I would normally be asleep. I would wander into my kitchen/living room where the table tennis table would be waiting. I would be wide awake and eager for an hour of hardcore but satisfying training with Ben. Then my day would return to normal. Basically, it would be no different to the year before, except that I would have utilised an hour I'd otherwise be asleep. 365 days later I'd have the skills of a table tennis pro.

Perhaps unsurprisingly, to everyone except me, it didn't turn out like that. Not even close. But despite the trips abroad, daily treks around London looking for competition and the often twice daily training; I was still managing to live a relatively normal life. My weekdays were full but at least on the weekends I could attempt to maintain my crumbling social life. That was until tournament season started.

From that first ever little tournament put on by Rory Scott on 8th November, right up until the final tournament on 11th January, every single weekend (except one) would be given up to go to a tournament. That's virtually two months without a weekend. We travelled to Horsham, Bristol, Slough, Nottingham, London, Cardiff, Harlow, Sussex and Slough (again). We didn't even get Christmas off! Christmas Day landed on a Thursday and was sandwiched with tournaments on either side.

My first official ranking tournament was in Bristol. We booked a Travelodge for the night before at a service station about half an hour from the venue. Ben wanted us to get there for 8 a.m. in the morning so that I could get a decent warm up and practice on the tables. I felt that was pretty early, as my matches weren't scheduled to start until 10:40, but Ben insisted it was necessary. I really had no idea what to expect so took his word for it. I tried and failed, to get some sleep and at the drowsy time of 6:30 a.m. we got up, grabbed some breakfast and headed to the centre.

We arrived at this massive hall at the University of West England. To one side was a tier of spectator seats while the rest of the hall was filled with table tennis tables, separated by plastic barriers with narrow walkways delineated in between. There were seats set out by each table for the players and coaches to use.

We were almost the first people there. As we started knocking up on the table, the place felt practically cavernous. There was hardly anyone around and it was completely silent apart from the sound of our ball bouncing on the table, echoing throughout the hall. Really Ben? Did we really need to get here this early? But then, like the floodgates had opened, players started sweeping into the hall. Before long all of the tables were full, and then any new player that arrived could only warm up through this archaic practice known as 'cross knocking'.

'Cross knocking' is probably the worst invention anyone in table tennis has ever come up with. The basic principle is that there aren't enough tables for everyone to warm up on, so instead you play four to a table. Each player stands diagonal to their partner and starts warming up, hitting the ball crosscourt and being careful not to let it stray into the other pair's 'zone'. It's horrible and really stressful. You can't move much for fear of getting in someone else's way. Occasionally the balls will clash in the middle. Joining us on our table were two top players, many leagues better than me, while here I was at my first ever tournament. They were perfectly polite but each time I got in their way I imagined them tutting at me.

"Who is this amateur? Out of my way noob!"

Ben was right. It is definitely worth getting there before everyone else and getting in some stress-free practice on your own table. Once the hall fills up and the tournament starts, there are almost no other chances.

As my matches started late, I was able to spend the first few hours watching and getting a feel for the setup. When you arrive you are registered and given a number which you wear on your back. Then you just sit around until you hear your name called on the tannoy. You might be umpiring or you might be playing.

"What happens if you don't hear your name?" I asked Ben. He looked at me like I was an idiot.

"Then they say it again until you do hear."

You generally play in two separate tournaments depending on how many ranking points you have. The band you deserve to be in and the one above. As I had no ranking points I was registered to play in Band 6 and Band 5. Band 5 had some players in it in the top 600 in England.

My initial Band 6 group only had three players, which meant that to progress through to the first round I only needed one victory. One player was really tough, a kid named Jay Ghazi-Timms who was one of the best in the country in his age group, but the other was an unranked player like me. They played each other first which gave me time to study their skills. The unranked player got battered.

"I can take him", I thought.

"You can take him", Ben said.

This was my first ever official match, and as I walked up to the table I was physically shaking with nerves. Something about sitting around waiting for hours had piled on the pressure. When we first arrived I was silently confident, I had watched my motivational video and was feeling good. But that was a long time earlier. Since then the nerves had crept up on me. To make it worse, we had Paul Stimpson, Table Tennis England's senior communications officer, taking notes for an article he would write about my first ever match. I'd spoken to Paul a few times, and he's a really lovely guy and a great journalist, but seeing him watching me and taking notes was really not helping.

I completely fluffed the first game. I couldn't seem to get any of my shots on the table. I was stiff, nervous and starting to doubt myself.

"Pull yourself together Sam". I muttered as I walked back to corner to talk to Ben. He just looked at me, it was clear he couldn't think what to say:

"You can beat him", was all he came up with. It was clear he wanted to tell me I was playing like a pansy but didn't want to push my nerves over the edge.

The second game started and slowly I got into it. My feeling improved, my shoulders relaxed and I started to fight back. I won that game. And the next. And the next. Boom! I had done it. I had won my first ever match at a ranking tournament, 3-1. Wow, I had made it through the group stages. Granted my victory was against another unranked player but I was feeling pretty great about it all. Well done Sam.

As expected I lost my group match against Jay (he was really good), and then I lost my first round match in the knockout phase too. I was drawn against Cade Short, the Welsh #3 at under 15 level. Even so, it was still a great start.

Walking around the hall after that match Ben bumped into Rory Scott (the guy who had put on the tournament the week before).

"How did Sam get on?" He asked, obviously expecting Ben to say that I had lost everything. After all what chance did I have if I was losing to everyone at a local tournament the week before?

"He got through the group stages," Ben replied, walking away from a speechless Rory.

It turns out you spend the majority of your time at a tournament waiting. You might get called to umpire a match, then you wait some more. Fortunately for me all the waiting and chatting to people bred familiarity. By the afternoon, and my Band 5 matches, I was very comfortable and almost enjoying myself. Again, I played quite well. I lost to two fairly strong players but had a good match against Mathew Pearce, a young boy who was ranked #10 in Wales at under 13 level. He won 3-2, but it was close run with two sets going to deuce that I could have won. I guess that gives you a rough idea of my level at the time. I lost 3-0 to the third best 15-year-old in Wales but was pretty 50/50 with the tenth best 13-year-old.

"You did really well," Ben told me on the trip home. "That was a really tough tournament".

I felt he was probably right. I had played six players and if I'm honest four of them had simply been too good for me. There was no point beating myself up over losing to strong, experienced players.

15

CRUNCH TIME

"I'm trying to stay as calm as possible and focus one day at a time, but when reality sets in, I feel everything: anxiety, excitement, nerves, pressure and joy." - Shawn Johnson

16th November 2014 – 11th January 2015

It felt like the standard at Bristol had been much higher than at the Medway Grand Prix we had watched in September. Where were all those low-level players I had been expecting to beat? But as we travelled up and down the country the majority of these beatable players never appeared again. I reckon they must have got discouraged early on in the season, and by the time I started playing events had already dropped out. It is not much fun giving up your weekends and travelling all over the country to competitions just to lose.

Tournament after tournament rolled by with very similar results. I would lose almost all my matches, and only picked up a few wins against other unranked players. Each week we could see me improving. I would be getting better and the videos started to look really good. I went from being an obvious outsider to looking much more at home. I would warm up with someone before a match and there'd be a grudging approval in their eyes. Unfortunately, this didn't show up on the score sheet.

After a tough time at major tournaments in Cippenham and Nottingham we decided I should sign up to a local one. I entered the second tier of the Highbury Winter Tournament. It wasn't part of the Table Tennis England circuit, and I wouldn't get any ranking points for winning matches, but I was feeling down and dejected, and I needed a confidence boost. The Highbury tournament would have a lot more amateur players entering and give me a chance to actually win some matches.

It was a much bigger tournament than the previous local tournament I had been to, I expect because it was based in London. Instead of the eight players at Horsham, there were just over 50 players in my tier. In that way, it felt like a cross between a Grand Prix and the Horsham tournament, but in experience it was entirely different to both. When playing top players in the Grand Prix's there was something about knowing that they should beat me, knowing I was the underdog, that made me feel like there was nothing to lose. But this was a tournament where I was up against a lot of players I was expected to beat. I'd never been in a situation like that before! Suddenly, I was playing against people where I should just be able to keep the ball on the table and win the match.

I got through the group stages pretty comfortably. Two of the four players in my group really struggled to return my serves, so they were very straightforward victories. The final player I came up against was quite good, but I was still expected to win. When warming up, an observer would have assumed I was the better, more dominant player. But during the game I fell apart. I was stiff, I didn't have faith in my abilities, and I went right back to doing those 'pansy' shots we had tried so hard to eradicate from my game. I lost. He beat me 3-2.

I was totally thrown. I walked over to where Ben was sitting and kind of shrugged. It didn't really matter as I still went through to the knockout stages, but losing to someone so early on really hammered my confidence - a confidence that never really came back. Confidence is so important in competitive table tennis. It's the reason a player can look awesome one moment and then awful the next. Sometimes you can see a player lose confidence right in the middle of a game and watch the momentum completely swing to their opponent.

I muddled my way through the first of the knockout stages, and then the one after. I wasn't getting any better and if anything I was just getting more nervous. Each round my opponent was getting tougher and my margin of victory was getting smaller.

"I don't know what's going on. I can't get any of my shots on. I'm missing everything! What should I do?" I asked Ben.

"I don't know. I don't know what sport you're playing out there, but it's certainly not the table tennis I've been teaching you". He replied.

I was through to the quarter-finals and my opponent was tough. I was at my most nervous so far but was pleasantly surprised to win the first two games quite easily. Then he seemed to figure out how to play me and I just fell apart. He dominated the next two, bringing the score in games to 2-2, meaning we had another final game to play, and everything to fight for. I paced up and down, delaying the start of the set for way too long.

"Come on Sam. Bully the ball. You can do it." I tried to big myself up in my head.

The game started and it was tight. We exchanged points, keeping level with each other all the way to 8-8. It was my turn to serve.

"I've got it!" I was thinking. "My serve is a strength and all I have to do is win these two points and then it will be really tough for him to come back."

I served, he did a weak return, and I tried to smash it - except, I missed. Crash into the net, the ball went. 8-9.

"Okay. No biggie," I was thinking. "Just get this one point and then you're still joint."

I served, straight into the net.

I don't think I have ever felt so bad in any table tennis game before or since, 8-9 in the fifth and final set, in the quarter-finals, and I had served into the net! I shouldn't be missing any serves, let alone one at such a crucial point. It was now 10-8 to him and it was his serve. I had pretty much lost. I had to win four straight points, whereas he only had to win one. But somehow, miraculously, I pulled it back. It went 10-9, 10-10, then 11-10 to me and finally, joyfully, 12-10. Game, set and match. I was through to the final four.

Unfortunately I lost in the semis, exiting the tournament in fourth place. It was quite a strange experience really. I had my best ever placing in a tournament and I even got a trophy for reaching the semi-finals. I had finished fourth out of about 50 players, even finishing above the person who beat me in the group stages, but our trip home was a subdued affair. We both knew I could have done better. We both knew that I hadn't played well despite my on-paper result. The competition in the Grand Prix's was on a whole different level to these local league players. I should have won that tournament.

The ranking tournaments continued and I continued struggling. It was depressing as I would travel all that way, get up so early and then spend the day losing to every ranked player I came up against. My improvement over those two months was really remarkable, but it just went to show how good some of these players were. How much at a level above me they were. The thing was there were a few ranked players around that we reckoned I could beat, but each tournament was a lucky dip. What would my draw be like? Would I be up against someone awesome I don't have a chance against, another unranked player, or would I be lucky enough to face somebody with ranking points that I could actually beat?

Table tennis has a very low variance when it comes to underdogs and upsets. Unlike team sports, it is very unusual for a better player to lose to a significantly weaker player. There are just too many chances over the five games of 11 points for the quality to show through. You can't really "get lucky" and fluke a win. At least, it doesn't happen very often. That meant if I had a tough draw, I was pretty much destined to lose. And I had some really tough groups.

My toughest group was in Band 5 at the Cardiff Grand Prix. Our four-man group consisted of Team GB Paralympian Paul Karabardak (who had won the Band 6 event that morning and has almost 15 years of International playing experience up his sleeve), Joshua Stacey (the Welsh #1 at under 15 level who went on to beat Paul Karabardak in their match), Mark Burridge (a Plymouth University player with an 87.5% average in the top division of the Exeter Table Tennis League), and me. I didn't stand a chance against Paul or Joshua. If I'm being honest I couldn't really expect to get anything from my match against Mark either but we had a really good game and I left happy despite losing 11-8, 11-8, 11-1. All the losing sucked, but it would have been disrespectful for me to get all angry about it. These guys I was up against were class players, with years of experience, and simply holding my own with them was an achievement in itself.

For our final tournament, Ben and I had entered as a team. It was a nice way to end the challenge and meant that provided at least one of us won our matches we would progress from the groups. It was also the first one where I had a mini crowd of supporters. All throughout the year friends and family had asked me if they could come and watch, but I always put it off.

"You can come along when I start winning." I would reply.

The problem was, I never started winning. The final tournament arrived and my family's invite didn't. Ben, on the other hand, had no qualms about his friends and family seeing my humiliation. His parents came to watch, as did his wife Katie, and a video producer called Joe who would be filming. This was only Katie's second ever table tennis tournament. I hoped that she'd have a better time than her first trip!

I was playing my best ever - the pinnacle of just over a year of daily training and coaching. I had a fantastic game against a guy called Ed Slot, who was a real top 250 player, getting painfully close to him in one set. I also played really well against another Welsh player called Neil Wright who has beaten Ben in many previous encounters. I always seemed to get drawn against the Welsh players for some reason.

My final match of the day, the final match of the year, was against Steve Smith, a player ranked about 500th in England. I knew it was a long shot but if I could beat him I would enter the ranking list just below him. Steve was an old hand, exactly the sort of player I wanted to come up against. He was stalwart, had been playing for many years, and grinded out his points through hard work. He wasn't a junior who didn't have many points because he rarely played senior tournaments - which was sadly my most common opponent. More than that, I actually felt like I had a chance against Steve. This could be it. My last chance for a fairy tale ending. An opportunity to get an impressive ranking in my final match of the final tournament.

The match got under way. Steve played a slow consistent game while I dived straight in, attacking regularly and trying to batter my way through his solid defence. It was close and he took the first game 11-9. I could see that Ben and the rest of my supporters were on the edge of their seats willing me on. It was so close. All I needed was a bit of luck. I would have taken all the nets and edges I could have got at that point. Steve took the second game as well. I was playing well, moving a lot and playing strong attacking shots, but I could feel it slipping through my fingers. The third and final game ended 11-7 to Steve.

He had won the match 3-0 and brought The Expert in a Year Challenge to a crashing end. Steve Smith had crushed my final hopes.

16

A RETURN TO NORMAL

"The only time you should ever look back is to see how far you've come." – Unknown

12th January – 22nd February 2015

The film Dodgeball calls itself 'A True Underdog Story'. Unfortunately, that isn't the case. If it had been a *true* underdog story the team of misfits from Average Joe's gym would have lost, again and again, to every and any team they came up against that actually knew what they were doing. That would have made for a rather depressing film, but it would have been more *true* to real life.

The film starts off realistic enough, with the Average Joe's dodgeball team being soundly defeated by a Girl Scout troop in a local qualifying match (I can relate). However, after going through on a technicality they improve rapidly. The team receives coaching from a dodgeball legend and with the good fortune to overcome numerous setbacks, and a belief that anything is possible, they go on to win the Las Vegas tournament and the

$50,000 prize. If only things were that easy.

When I arrived home from my final tournament (at about 7 p.m. on a Sunday evening) I was crushed - it had been a long 12 months. Back in January I'd been excited and optimistic about mastering a new skill and breaking into the upper echelon of English table tennis, but as the year had progressed the likelihood of success had diminished and now it had vanished completely. I had put in so much work. I couldn't have done any more.

Originally, the plan had been to do an hour of table tennis a day in my kitchen, but in the end I clocked up over 500 hours of table tennis practice. I'd probably spent another 500 hours travelling and getting ready for sessions (or showering afterwards). I'd worked with at least 15 different coaches and had trained in Malta, Denmark and Hungary, and in Middlesbrough on three occasions. For the last eight weeks, I had sacrificed every weekend going up and down the country for tournaments. It had completely taken over my life.

It would have all been worth it if we'd achieved our goal, but we hadn't. After all that work; I'd failed.

I was still nowhere near the top 250 target. I hadn't even come close. It wasn't like I'd finished with a ranking of 300th - close but not quite there. I wasn't even good enough to get an official ranking. Over those last eight weeks, I must have played about 30 ranked table tennis players, and I couldn't beat any of them. The few matches I had won were against other players in a similar position to me; players who were trying, and failing, to get a ranking.

Worse, it was the most public failure ever. I had told everyone I'd met about what we were doing and Ben had posted it all over the internet. I'm sure there were a lot of people that wanted to say, "I told you so." Many had said it was an impossible task and we had proved them right. I don't think Ben ever honestly believed I could become a top 250 player in a year, but I think he thought I'd finish somewhere, with something to show for all the hard work we'd put in.

From the moment I started playing tournaments, my whole aim had been simply to beat any player with a ranking - just one. I really wanted to get a ranking - any ranking. I would have taken being right at the bottom of the list as long as I could have told people, "Hi, I'm Sam Priestley and I'm ranked number 842 in England for table tennis." It would have been something. But I hadn't got my win and I had nothing to show for all the effort I had put in. Sure, I could now beat Toby and Dan easily but I hadn't made much of a dent on the world of competitive table tennis.

Had I completely wasted the past year? Does everyone now think I'm a loser? Should I just go and curl up, cry, and eat pizza and Ben & Jerry's ice cream?

Those were just some of the thoughts running through my mind as I reflected on the challenge - and I did eat my fair share of Ben & Jerry's. I decided I was going to stop playing table tennis completely for a few weeks and then see if I wanted to continue playing, obviously a lot less frequently, or simply give it up altogether - I was still part of one of the ISH teams playing in the Central London League so there were matches to play if I wanted to.

While I was down in dumps, keeping Domino's Pizza in business, Ben was busy working on a compilation video of my year of table tennis. He took one-second clips from every day of the challenge and strung them together into a 1 Second Everyday-style montage. He finished it and uploaded it to YouTube on 13th January 2015, two days after the end of the challenge. It was titled 'Guy Plays Table Tennis Every Day for a Year' - descriptive.

The video was great. It was a nice reminder of some of the highs and lows of the past 12 months and clearly showed how much I had improved. Before the training began I looked so wooden and awkward. By the end of the video, I was holding my own against a serious player at an official ranking tournament. I must have watched it through at least ten times and it did make me feel a lot better.

It reminded me how much I had enjoyed the process. And I did really enjoy it - honest. It was an incredible experience. For one thing, I can't quite believe I saw it all through - a whole year of table tennis. I don't think I've ever made such a big commitment in my life. I'm certain some of my friends and family expected me to pack it in part way through.

I had met some pretty amazing people too. First there were the true experts in their fields, guys like Mario Genovese in Malta and Lei Yang and Istvan Moldovan in Denmark. These men had all played and coached table tennis at the highest international level and had a wealth of knowledge to share. It's not every day you get access to such high achievers. Then there were all the other friends I made along the way; people that helped me like Mark Simpson and Steve Brunskill, club mates at ISH like Zeshi and Paul. There are too many to mention. The whole table tennis community was really supportive too. Every time I went to a tournament people would come up to me and say "good luck" and that they had been following my weekly videos. In Denmark, a couple of Scandinavian juniors came up to me saying they'd been watching me on YouTube. It meant a lot.

I even saw snooker legend Ronnie O'Sullivan at a tournament - he was inadvertently watching my match against Josh Dye at the BATTS Super Series. And I played the actor Roderic Culver (he was in V for Vendetta and 28 Weeks Later) in a local league match during the final week of the challenge. I beat him 3-0. I wish I'd got that on video!

Over the next few weeks, my montage video clocked up about 8,000 views and we were both pretty happy. We had a small core group of table tennis fans who had been following my progress and their response was very positive.

I decided to start playing in the local league again on 10th February. I felt a bit rusty as I wasn't used to having to compete without practicing every day. I decided I needed to practice with someone more my level and found a new practice partner at Morpeth TTC in East London. I started going there once a week for a couple of hours.

My long-term plan was to work my way up the Central London Table Tennis divisions slowly but surely. I was going to try and get myself into a division four team for the 2015/16 season and then hopefully into division three the year after. I was perfectly happy to continue playing once a week and get some use out of the skills I had developed. Playing in the lower division would mean I'd be winning most of my matches as well – a much more enjoyable experience. I ended up winning eight out of nine of my matches, losing one 11-9 in the fifth.

The Expert in a Year Challenge had come to an end, all the videos had been uploaded, and we were both getting used to having a fair amount of extra free time in the week. As far as I was concerned, that was the end of it.

****

Bzzzzzzt. Bzzzzzt. Bzzzzt.

As I slowly gained consciousness, I blinked bleary eyed at my phone. 3 a.m., the phone said. You have 10 new Facebook notifications.

It was 17th February - just over a month since we'd finished the challenge. The messages were from someone I didn't even know; a guy called Dan Seemiller. I unlocked my phone to see what he was saying:

"Hi, I found your video and posted it to Reddit so more people could see it. It's got about 2k more views since I posted it and here's the thread for it... Cheers!"

That's pretty cool, I thought. We had spoken about posting something on Reddit but had never actually got round to it. The link said, "88 points and 25 comments so far". By the time I clicked over to the website, it had grown to over 50 comments. I read through them all, refreshed the page, and read through the new ones.

There was no going back to sleep now. I sat in bed refreshing the page for a couple of hours and then at 5:15 a.m. I text Ben.

"It's literally going mental!!"

"The video has gone from 8k views to 15k views"

"In like 4 hours"

Now that's low expectations for you! Four days later we had over a million views. Those four days were pretty mad.

When Ben got up in the morning there were a bunch of emails waiting for him from various media agencies and news sites, some asking to do interviews, a couple trying to buy the rights for the video, and even one asking us to go on Swedish television. The video only had about 50,000 views at that point, but it was being picked up by journalists and reporters from all over the place. It was pretty exciting. We were everywhere. On 17th February 2015 Ben and I were the guys everyone wanted to talk to. We did phone interviews that morning with people from the BBC and The Telegraph, refreshing the video every few minutes as we saw the number of views shoot upwards.

At first I wasn't sure what to say to these people. After all, it wasn't like we'd achieved our target. They would ask me what my ranking was now and I would have to sheepishly say that I hadn't actually managed to get one. I was worried they might say something like;

"Oh, sorry. I thought you had gone from nothing to top 250 in a year. But you didn't even manage to get an England ranking? What's the story here? Why am I talking to you?"

But it wasn't like that at all. People didn't see it as a failure. They couldn't care less about whether I'd reached number 250 or not because they were much more interested in what I had accomplished. I was the first to admit that I hadn't managed to reach Ben's 'expert' level but to them that didn't matter. They had seen the video with their own eyes and as far as they were concerned I was awesome at table tennis. I had transformed myself in just one year.

Some of the journalists got a bit carried away (one even referred to me as an "unstoppable champ") but the prevailing response was one of congratulations. None said, 'You're not really *that* good at table tennis." Every non-table-tennis-playing journalist that watched me prance around playing ping pong agreed that I had got really good, very quickly. Despite failing to reach our ambitious target the fact that I was now a 'good' table tennis player was never questioned.

As someone who was clearly pretty awful at table tennis at the beginning, my transformation had shown people that 'unsporty' or 'uncoordinated' doesn't have to be a label for life. If you want to, you can change it. I was living proof that dedication and plenty of practice pays off, eventually. But it doesn't happen overnight. In fact, I began to realise that not reaching our target may have even been a good thing. I received this comment after the end of the challenge from a fellow table tennis player who had been at it for many years;

"If you had actually succeeded at getting into the top 250, I would have felt terrible. I have been trying to improve myself over all these years and still haven't yet reached that level."

Instead of making him feel terrible, the challenge had shown that learning the correct technique and dramatically improving your game is possible for anyone. But at the same time it really shone a spotlight on to how hard working and deserving the 'experts' at table tennis really are. They've put in years of dedication to reach that level – their 10,000 hours of deliberate practice.

The next thing that happened took us by surprise too. "I want to do my own Expert in a Year", is what we began to see popping both from other table tennis players and from the wider internet. We were both receiving emails from complete strangers that said they loved the 'Expert in a Year' idea and wanted to do something similar.

In a lot of ways, Ben's challenge had succeeded. He showed that with enough practice you can take a random person and get them to a decent level. I hadn't improved 10x faster than the average player, but I had got very good for just one years worth of training. Even better, it looked like my progress had inspired other table tennis players to start training harder too. For me, that made the whole year of hard work, early starts and very little free time 100% worth it.

REFLECTIONS

It's now just over six months since I finished The Expert in a Year Challenge – well, the table tennis one at least. I've started another one and I'm learning Brazilian Jiu Jitsu, a sport I didn't know anything about until a couple of months ago. Ben's doing his own Marathon in a Year Challenge too, but that's another story altogether.

My year of table tennis was certainly an experience. It's taken some time to really sink in. I learnt a lot from The Expert in a Year Challenge, and not just about table tennis. I feel like I received a first-class education in goal setting, discovered the truth about mastery, and unearthed things about myself I didn't even realise existed. It was a long journey but one that taught me much more than any book or course possibly could. My whole outlook on success has completely changed.

Looking back it's obvious that the challenge was pretty much unachievable, and it's just as clear that Ben knew it. I was incredibly naive when it came to everything table tennis in 2013 and I had no idea how tough it was going to be. Thinking back, it seems almost arrogant of me to be strutting around telling people I was going to get into the top 250 players in England in just a year, only sacrificing a measly hour a day. But as offensive as it was to the established table tennis world, I now understand that that ridiculous goal was essential.

Ben was clever not to ask me, "Do you fancy playing table tennis every day for a year, and when you finish you'll probably be a bit better than you are now?" I would have told him where to go! After all, if your dream is uninspiring you are much more likely to quit - or never even start. I doubt I would have achieved half as much with a more 'realistic' goal. I would have slacked off and taken it easy. My overly ambitious target kept me on my toes and enabled me to get closer to my potential. It reminds me of that famous quote by W. Clement Stone;

"Aim for the moon. If you miss, you may hit a star."

I may have failed to reach the goal we set but, for an uncoordinated computer geek, I still got pretty darn good at table tennis. Speaking of failure, that reminds me of another quote I like;

"Success consists of going from failure to failure without loss of enthusiasm." – Winston Churchill.

Failing is never easy. In fact, the reason most people don't try to achieve things is because 'if you don't try, you can't fail'. It's a defense mechanism for our ego and a pretty good one too - personally, I've never failed at something I haven't tried. But I've learnt that failure is simply part of the journey and, as someone who has failed extremely publicly, I can assure you that it really isn't as bad as you would think. Failure is not fatal.

In reality, the only thing at stake is your pride, and a small amount of time. Yeah, it's a little bit embarrassing but personally I'd rather aim a bit too high, give it my all and fail publicly, than do another secret rowing style challenge, give up, achieve nothing and tell no one. Even if you fail, there is something noble in trying.

What we are all striving for in these endeavours is mastery. True mastery, the quest for perfection, remains beyond one's grasp, but I've realised that basic mastery is achievable for all. Since finishing the year I've coined my own little phrase;

"Mastery is tough, but mastery is possible."

To me that means; there are no shortcuts to mastery, you need to put in the work. But if you put in the work, anything is possible. And there were definitely times in the year when the going got tough, really tough. It wasn't all smooth sailing. I wasn't always a happy bunny.

This is such an important lesson and has meaning far beyond table tennis. The value of hard work is just as true in academic studies, music, business, and all areas of life. Slacking off, quitting, spending hours procrastinating and searching for the latest shortcut or 'magic pill' isn't going to get you anywhere. We all need to accept that mastery is tough and takes time.

Talking about shortcuts; I've spent a bit of time recently trying to work out what the Tim Ferriss approach to table tennis would be. What would be his hack to get pretty good, very fast? I reckon it would be heavy backspin. If you have no intention of actually becoming a competitive table tennis player, and only want to find a way to beat the majority of people without putting in hours of work yourself, I think learning how to create heavy backspin would be the answer. If you got a bat with decent rubbers that could actually generate spin and then spent a few days or so getting very good at playing with heavy backspin, I reckon that would be enough to beat most of your friends. That would probably be the fastest way to start seeing significant results in your matches. The best 'hack'.

But, of course, that only works up to a level. There's a reason a top 250 player can beat me on autopilot; they've put in thousands of hours of practice over many years to rewire their brains and bodies with high-level table tennis circuitry. To think you can beat them by mastering one shot is ridiculous because, as I painfully discovered, even after 12 whole months of hardcore deliberate training you still won't stand a chance against the top boys.

It took US player Alex Polyakov, author of Breaking 2000, two and a half years to reach a 2000 rating (and we estimate top 250 in England is roughly a 2100 USATT rating). The most dedicated and 'talented' English junior players don't usually manage to break into the top 250 until they are at least 14 years old, after several years of training and competing. From talking to a number of different table tennis coaches and players we reckon, realistically, it would take me another two years of daily training, at least, to reach our initial top 250 target, probably more. As much as I enjoyed my year of table tennis I don't fancy doing another two or three years of it. I'm happy to take it easy from now on and play for fun and for ISH in the Central London League. I'm in no rush and I'm it for the long haul. Perhaps my favourite thing about table tennis is that you can you can play it for most of your life. During the challenge I got beaten by a 10-year-old and by a 90-year-old. I plan to be that 90-year-old.

I'm guessing – seeing as you've got this far through our book – that you're really into table tennis, and do want to put in the work required to get really good. If so, I'd like to take this opportunity to encourage you to keep going. No matter your current level or age I now believe wholeheartedly that anyone can significantly improve their performance, in a relatively short period of time, as long as they are willing to put the work in and do plenty of table tennis practice. Sure, 'talent' probably has some sort of effect on how good you can potentially get, or how quickly you'll improve, but I wouldn't worry about it too much. Just focus on making daily improvements and try to surround yourself with good players and coaches that you can learn from.

During my year of table tennis, I learnt a number of important lessons (some theoretical, some practical). I would like to share them with you now. I hope they help you to achieve everything you want to in this fascinating sport. I've also included some of my favourite quotes that helped motivate me along the way.

1. Turn It Into A Thing

"The main thing is to keep the main thing the main thing" - Stephen Covey

You could argue that The Expert in a Year Challenge, and especially our top 250 goal, caused me a lot of stress and anxiety that the average table tennis player doesn't have to deal with. It certainly put me under pressure to perform. It also meant that I often didn't fully appreciate my small victories because they were so insignificant relative to our long-term target. We probably could have dealt with some of that a little better.

However, I know how important turning my table tennis into a 'thing' was. If it hadn't of been given a name and shared publicly I almost certainly would have given up somewhere along the line. The 'year' part of it gave me a finish line to look ahead to and a reason to keep going when times were tough. The 'expert' part kept my focus on a really high level of play and stopped me from settling for anything sub-par. Altogether, there was no possibility of being distracted along the way by something new and more exciting.

In the future, if I ever want to achieve anything important, I will definitely spend a bit of time coming up with a plan and turning it into some sort of challenge.

2. Prioritise Your Table Tennis

"I suppose the biggest change really is the priorities in my life. To be a top athlete you do have to, at times, be quite selfish but now I have to always consider my girls." - Mo Farah

After the challenge had finished, just for fun, Ben decided to work out exactly how many days during 2014 I didn't play table tennis on (he's strange like that). After he had his answer he sent me a text message and asked me to guess. "35?" I replied. I was way off! It turns out I actually had 95 rest days during the year. That's 95 days out of 365 where I didn't even pick up my bat. I was shocked. The point is this; you need to prioritise your table tennis.

There is always a good reason not to practice; holidays, parties, family stuff, other commitments, meetings. Some of the time you need to be selfish and put your table tennis before other people and things. Other times you need to make sacrifices and choose table tennis over something else you'd rather be doing. The top players prioritise their table tennis and reap the rewards.

The funny thing is, we *did* prioritise my table tennis in 2014 and I still had loads and loads of days off. Imagine how little table tennis I would have played if we hadn't of been taking it so seriously!

3. Don't Break The Chain

"Without routine you're lost; you're not going to achieve anything." -
Ronnie O'Sullivan

When it comes to actually getting in those all-important practice sessions, it really comes down to creating positive habits and a solid routine. You need to plan your training timetable well in advance so that you know that on this day, you are training at this time, at this club, and with this practice partner. Don't leave it to chance or try to sort things out on the day.

I really like the 'Don't break the chain' idea, which is credited to comedian Jerry Seinfeld. It's a very simple concept; decide you want to do something every day and then start marking off days on a wall calendar when you actually do it. After a few consecutive days of work you'll begin to form a chain and your job is to keep going every day so that you don't break it.

Of course, you'll miss days from time to time, but it's a good way of keeping track of exactly how much practice you are doing. It's easy to assume you are doing more than you actually are.

4. Join A Club

"If you want to go fast, go alone. If you want to go far, go together." -
African Proverb

I went along to ISH for the first time on Sunday 25th May 2014, almost five months into the challenge! I should have gone after the first week.

I believe Ben had this image in his mind where he would train me up for a few months in the kitchen and then, when he thought I was ready, release me into the world of club table tennis and watch me immediately start defeating players who had been playing for years due to my technical brilliance. That isn't how it works though. We both know that now. Part of becoming a good player is learning how to win - how to play against all sorts of different players – and you can't learn that in one-to-one coaching sessions.

There is no reason not to join a club as soon as possible. Ideally, try to find one that has a coach and offers structured training sessions that you can attend. But if you can't, any place where you can play against a variety of players is good enough. You cannot become a truly exceptional player if you limit yourself to solely one-to-one training or playing against a robot. You need to get out there into the 'real world'.

5. Find A Coach

"A coach is someone who tells you what you don't want to hear, who has you see what you don't want to see, so you can be who you have always known you could be." - Tom Landry

I was fortunate enough to have a coach guiding me through the entire process. I realise that most adult starters aren't that lucky. Some of the guys I met at ISH at the Sunday evening practice had been playing for years and had never even encountered a coach.

If you are an adult starter you probably aren't going to have coaches falling over themselves to begin coaching you - unfortunately, they all seem much more interested in working with the kids. However, you can still get access to high-quality coaching if you are prepared to pay for it.

In London, an hour of one-to-one coaching, with a decent coach, will probably cost you about £30. That might sound expensive, but it is worth it. A good coach will be able to save you from wasting so much time figuring things out or going down the wrong path altogether. An hour a week is plenty and you can even ask the coach to give you drills to work on during the week in between your sessions.

6. Go On Training Camps

"I hated every minute of training, but I said, 'Don't quit. Suffer now and live the rest of your life as a champion.'" - Muhammad Ali

I went on a lot of training camps during the challenge; I did three at Swerve in Middlesbrough, one with Eli Baraty in London, and two big ones abroad. They were really valuable and had some of the biggest effects on my table tennis of the whole year.

If you are used to playing just a few hours of table tennis a week then an intensive training camp gives you the opportunity to get in close to a month's worth of training in just a couple of days! On top of that you'll be surrounded by other players striving to improve and coaches ready to offer their advice. They don't cost as much as you'd think either.

Hardly anyone I met at the adult clubs I visited each week in London (ISH, Highbury and Finsbury) had ever gone on a training camp. I have no idea why – they would love it. Perhaps they just didn't know about them. If you are keen to improve your table tennis and haven't been on a camp you are missing out.

7. Get Used To Playing Kids

"Age is an issue of mind over matter. If you don't mind, it doesn't matter." - Mark Twain

As an adult man, I found it pretty weird going on training camps where the average age was about 13. It's just a situation that you don't really experience anywhere else in life. At first I felt a bit like I shouldn't be there – like I was hijacking their session.

You get used to it though. Unfortunately, there just aren't many places for you to go to receive good table tennis coaching, without being surrounded by kids. Strangely, I've found the complete opposite in Brazilian Jiu-Jitsu, where most of the beginners I train with are adults and it seems quite normal to take up the sport later in life and still take it very seriously.

The other thing you need to get over is playing matches against kids. Do you play your best? Is it okay to play the ball really short where their short arms can't reach it? Should you celebrate when you win a good point?

I know a lot of players struggle in matches against young children but after a while you begin to see past their age and view everyone based on their ability level. You can be proud of beating a 10 year old, if that 10 year old is one of the best in the country for his age group. That's just how you have to see it.

8. Relax

"Be like a duck. Calm on the surface, but always paddling like the dickens underneath." - Michael Caine

This one is really hard to do. Ben spent so much time telling me to 'relax' and it took me months to finally figure out what he meant - most of the time this was in training as well. My only real experience of serious sports training before the challenge was rowing - and there is no time for relaxation there. I was used to tensing up, narrowing my focus, and pushing through the pain barrier for a few minutes until the work was done.

Table tennis is completely different though, and that kind of mindset isn't going to get you anywhere. Your muscles need to be relaxed so that they can move quickly, react and make loads of minute adjustments. Your brain needs to be relaxed so that you can watch your opponent and take in all of the necessary information.

Your training, therefore, should adopt this relaxed approach somewhat. You need to develop the awareness of being relaxed and calm in your practice so that when you compete it comes naturally. Getting the balance right between training hard, but at the same time being relaxed, must be one of the hardest parts of the sport.

9. Try Shadow Play

*"I've always considered myself to be just average talent and what I
have is a ridiculous insane obsessiveness for practice and
preparation." - Will Smith*

I had never heard of shadow play before Ben came round
for my first training session on January 1st. Initially I didn't
like it - I felt awkward doing it and every time Ben
suggested it I thought he was saying I wasn't good enough
to be trusted with a real ball – but eventually I grew to love
it.

There is a book called The Talent Code by the author
Daniel Coyle which is quite similar to Bounce by Matthew
Syed. For the book, Coyle goes around the world visiting
these talent hotspots – one of which is Spartak Tennis
Club in Moscow, a club that has in recent years produced
more top-20 women players than the entire United States.

At Spartak, they do a lot of shadow play (they call it
imitatsiya) and it clearly gets results. The young children do
imitatsiya and the professional players do it as a warm up
before their practice sessions. They even go as far as to say
the ball is a distraction! The focus is on firing the circuit
and getting the action perfect. Then you add the ball.

I reckon table tennis could do with more imitatsiya. I
bet they do it in China.

10. Don't Rush The Fundamentals

*"Success is neither magical nor mysterious. Success is the natural
consequence of consistently applying the basic fundamentals." - Jim
Rohn*

When it comes to what to actually practice, by the end of
the year we had both realised the importance of the
fundamentals for long-term success. We skipped over
these way too fast in an attempt to move on to bigger and
better things. That was a massive mistake!

Ben has since admitted that he thought I wouldn't stand a chance of winning matches at tournaments unless I could open-up, counter loop, flick, and do all sorts of other advanced techniques and tactics. But now he has changed his mind. Whereas we went about making sure I was able to do everything moderately well, Ben now thinks I would have actually won more matches if we had stuck to the basics and not got to a lot of the trickier stuff.

If I had concentrated on perfecting the drive, push, block and topspin, and spent the year working on my consistency and placement (instead of power and aggressiveness) I probably would have made a lot less mistakes and played much better table tennis. It wouldn't have been as flashy to watch but it would have been more effective.

The other point that really shocked me was the importance of pre-fundamental 'sporty' skills such as balance, coordination and agility for table tennis. I've never been very good at these but assumed it wouldn't matter – how wrong I was! If I'd spent a bit more time working specifically on these during the first half of the year I probably would have felt a lot more natural and comfortable with my techniques.

11. Learn Spin First

"He who would learn to fly one day must first learn to stand and walk and run and climb and dance; one cannot fly into flying." - Friedrich Nietzsche

Table tennis is a spin game. If you understand how to generate spin, and deal with your opponent's spin, you are going to do well. If you allow spin to bamboozle you, you are in big trouble.

I remember discussing spin with Ben quite early on. We both decided that mastering spin was really difficult and could take years and therefore attempting to do so would be a bad strategy. We decided to focus on power instead, which we believed to be my 'unfair advantage' over my competition. Again – this was stupid.

Now we actually reckon that it is a big advantage for kids to be lacking in power when they start playing the game because it forces them to learn to use spin to win points. Watch any U13 match and you'll see long rallies where the winner uses spin and placement to outwit his opponent. They don't have the power required to hit a massive third ball winner so they have to develop an all-round game. This stands them in very good stead later on when they do start to add some power to their shots.

Spin is fundamental and the earlier you start learning how it works the better. I found our switching drill the most useful way to get my head around how to control the ball with spin, but the key take-away is to experiment, slow the ball down, and try things out. Have fun with it. This kind of deliberate play is essential.

12. Practice Your Serves

"The beginning is the most important part of the work." - Plato

I can't blame Ben for this one – service practice is just plain boring. I had a table in my flat, and plenty of balls, so there was really no excuse for not doing some service practice every day. I just didn't.

Most people don't. I asked quite a few people over the year if they did any service practice and hardly anyone did. Everyone knows it is important but yet nobody can bring themselves to do it. Lei Yang was the exception. He thought 90 minutes a day was a reasonable amount!

I doubt any of us have the time, or patience, to do 90 minutes of service practice a day but if you really want to get good at table tennis you should be doing as much as possible. 15 minutes is what I aimed for. Your serve is a closed skill – meaning you have complete control over it – and therefore there should be no reason for not having awesome serves (at least compared to your level of competition).

A great serve makes it so much easier to get your strengths into the game. If you have a good open-up you need a really good backspin serve that forces your opponent to give you a push. If you prefer a fast game you should work on perfecting a disguised fast serve to catch your opponent out and set you up for a third ball attack. Actually, learn both of those and that's a pretty good start.

13. Work On Defense Too

"Basketball is like war in that offensive weapons are developed first, and it always takes a while for the defense to catch up." - Red Auerbach

Early on in the challenge we decided that I should become an all-out attacking player. Any passive or defensive shots were thrown in the bin. This was a ginormous mistake.

Playing the majority of my table tennis in one-to-one coaching sessions was already enough to make it difficult for me to work on my defense – because I didn't have to control the ball for my opponent's drills – but what we did made it even worse. I was never any good at blocking or controlling the ball and it really held me back.

We both understand now how important it is to work on both the offensive and defensive parts of your game. Even if you are the type of player that wants to attack first and be aggressive, there are still going to be plenty of times when your opponent is attacking at you. If you aren't able to keep the ball on the table, and use placement or variation to force them to give you a ball that you can attack, then you are going to struggle big time.

Another benefit of being able to block is knowing you can practice with better players without being embarrassed or feeling like they don't want to play with you. If you are a good blocker more experienced players will be much happier to train with you.

14. Bully The Ball

"Make up your mind to act decidedly and take the consequences. No good is ever done in this world by hesitation." - Thomas Huxley

For a few months, this was my personal motto. "Bully the ball", I'd say to myself in the gaps between points. In the end, we decided that there was more to table tennis than simply committing to a shot and going for it – but it certainly helped me at the time. If you are the kind of player that often hesitates before making a decision and is uncertain about which shot to play then I reckon thinking about bullying the ball could really help you.

The thing is, to an extent, if you really go for a big forehand loop – and you get the technique, timing and contact all right – then you should be able to make the ball do whatever you want it to do. As a beginner, I found that I gave the spin on the ball too much respect. I would be thinking, "Where does the ball want to go?", too much and worrying about what the ball would let me do to it. After a while, once you've got the shots, you'll learn that you can pretty much tell the ball what to do if you hit it right. That is what the top players do.

Of course, you'll still need to understand what spin is on the ball and where it would naturally go if you allowed it to just hit your bat, but you'll realise that you have more power over the ball than you think. As I said earlier in the book, this one tip had an immediate effect on my performance in matches.

15. Be Match Specific

"Without Knowledge, action is useless and knowledge without action is futile." - Abu Bakr

This was the big take away from my time in Denmark, and, in particular, a training session I had with Istvan Moldovan. He was a master at planning practice that had a specific match-relevant outcome.

Istvan had a term he used to describe the kind of player who is always practicing but doesn't link the practice to their competitive experiences – technique freaks! He believed there was no point spending hours on improving the technique of a certain stroke if it wasn't going to make any noticeable difference to your performance. To me, this made a lot of sense.

One of Istvan's ideas was to make sure practically every drill starts with a serve and return of serve. Every point in a match begins in this way so it makes sense to get used to it in practice. You'd be surprised how many players hardly ever do this though. It is so much easier just to start a practice drill by hitting the ball into play and not having to deal with the annoying spin and variability of a serve.

16. Tactical Training Is Important Too

"Tactics mean doing what you can with what you have." - Saul Alinsky

In many ways technical training is the simplest form of training. Broadly speaking there is a correct and incorrect way to play each stroke and it is clear to see when you are making progress because you look better. What I mean is; technical training is quite tangible.

Tactical training, on the other hand, is intangible.

Watch a hall full of players training and it is pretty much impossible to spot who is tactically strong and who is tactically weak. Tactics are just as important as technique – perhaps even more important – but they are much easier to ignore.

You should make sure you spend a significant amount of your practice time thinking about tactics. We probably didn't do this enough. This tactical training can take the form of creating set pieces to use in matches, or thinking through the best shots to play in specific situations, or even watching top players' matches to observe the decisions they make. Then you need to get on the table and drill these into your subconscious so that you are able to make the correct decision automatically when it matters.

A big part of this is placement. Watch the top players and they are able to play shots into great positions even when they are being pushed to the max. Watch a bunch of amateur players and you'll see that they aren't even thinking about where they play their shots and perhaps even hit every single forehand loop they play crosscourt, straight into their opponents block.

17. Do A Proper Warm-Up

"If you spend too much time warming up, you'll miss the race. If you don't warm up at all, you may not finish the race." - Grand Heidrich

Ben loves getting to tournaments ridiculously early. At the Bristol Grand Prix, he made me arrive at 8 a.m. when my matches didn't start until 10:40! I understand it though. It can be really hard to get in a proper warm up when the tournaments are so busy and without a good warm up you are basically giving your opponent a huge advantage over you.

So, what kind of warm up should you do? Well, it's a

good idea to start with a bit of jogging and sidestepping away from the table – something to get your muscles warm and your heart rate up. Then you need to get yourself onto the table and use the time you have the best you can. You might want to spend a bit of time hitting forehands and backhands but make sure you also practice plenty of serves and return of serves. If you have the time you could even try doing some of your favourite practice drills to get you feeling really sharp.

Sometimes at a tournament I found myself sitting around for three hours or so in between matches. It's important to try and keep practicing during these long breaks otherwise you start to feel very lethargic and bored.

18. Everybody Gets Nervous

"I'm scared every time I go into the ring, but it's how you handle it. What you have to do is plant your feet, bite down on your mouthpiece and say, 'Let's go.'" - Mike Tyson

At my first ever tournament in Horsham, I was so nervous warming up with Ben that I could hardly keep the ball on the table. The week after, at Bristol, I could feel my body physically shaking during the first set of my first match and I fluffed it big time.

Those butterflies in your stomach before a match feel horrible, but it's important to remember that everybody gets nervous – it's part of being human. I know that Ben still gets nervous at tournaments and he's been playing for about 15 years. Even the professional players get nervous before big matches and they do this for a job.

If you feel yourself starting to panic I found it helpful to take my time, relax my muscles and breathe. Try to focus on your game plan and don't put too much pressure on yourself. All you can do is give it your best.

19. Attack Early In The Match

"The best defense is a good offense." - Proverb

When I was super nervous 'pansy table tennis' would rear its head and I'd find myself unable to do anything but pat and prod at the ball, terrified of making a mistake. I had my worst episodes of pansy table tennis in the local Highbury tournament I played in in December and in my match against Steve Hirst in January. In both instances I remember my mindset being, "Don't mess up. Don't make mistakes." This is a recipe for disaster.

I did come up with a decent strategy for dealing with it though; attack early on. I found that if I went out there attacking from the first point then I would find myself relaxing and settling into the game. Then, if I decided I was missing too many I could tone it down a bit later on, and if I was playing well I could just keep at it. On the other hand, if I started a game negatively, keeping the ball on the table and trying not to miss, I found that I simply couldn't start attacking later on. I had paralysed myself.

That's when things would get really bad. In some situations, I knew that I needed to start attacking a bit more, but my confidence had completely vanished and I was left pushing and pansy-ing. I hated myself in those moments.

20. A Win Is A Win

"A competitor will find a way to win." - Nancy Lopez

Ben spent a lot of the year telling me that it didn't matter if I won or lost my games, what was important was that I played correctly, made the right decisions, and was positive. I get what he was saying – he wanted me not to worry about winning and losing (which isn't directly in my control) and instead focus on my own performance. Too often though I came away from a match I had won unhappy because I hadn't managed to be as attacking as we'd wanted me to be.

After a while, I decided that a win is a win, and I should be happy with it. After all, the whole point of playing a sport is to win. People might say that it isn't, but it is. And it's a sad situation where you win a match and come away feeling awful about it.

Now that isn't to say that you can't learn things from matches you won playing badly but ultimately you can't always play your best in every match and if you can come away with a win, even when you weren't playing that well, then surely that's a result. That's what the professionals talk about. The best players can win matches and get through to the next round even when they aren't feeling great and things aren't 'clicking'.

21. Losing Is Inevitable

"First, accept sadness. Realize that without losing, winning isn't so great." - Alyssa Milano

This was something that Steve Brunskill said to us in one of his seminars back in February. There are some sports, like boxing, where top athletes can go undefeated for years at a time. Table tennis isn't like that. Even the world no.1 loses loads of matches during a season. And if you're not the world no.1 you are likely to lose a lot more than that! This means how you deal with your losses is really important.

I hate losing. During the challenge, I lost to ten-year-old kids. I lost to old men. I lost to Ben playing left-handed over and over again. I lost to my housemates Toby and Dan on occasion. The key is to learn from your losses.

Why did I lose? How can I stop it from happening again? What was letting me down? What were they doing that was causing me problems? These are the kinds of questions you need to be asking yourself.

I also learnt the importance of match selection. I lost a lot of tournament matches during the year and it really started to knock my confidence. It is no good losing over-and-over again because you end up stuck in the habit of losing and you walk onto the table expecting to lose every match. Especially when you are starting out I think you are better off playing in the lowest league division possible, against the weakest players. That's why I joined a team in Division 5 of the Central London League. You can experiment with different things, and learn just as much, when winning - and it is a lot more enjoyable.

22. Practice, Reflect, Learn, Repeat

"Learning without reflection is a waste. Reflection without learning is dangerous." - Confucius

The key to all of this is to keep learning. Learn in your training sessions. Learn from watching others. Learn from your wins. Learn from your losses. As long as you can take something away from a practice or tournament then it hasn't been a waste of time.

You also need to take ownership of your own improvement. During the challenge, I learnt how important it is for me to know what I need to work on in my practice sessions, and why. It was my responsibility to watch back old videos and check that I was doing what I thought I was doing.

In effect, you need to become your own coach. This is rather tricky when you don't know anything about table tennis, so you need to start learning. I must have spent hours online watching videos and reading articles. I'm doing the same for my Brazilian Jiu-Jitsu now as well. By the end of the challenge, I felt like I would have been able to coach a beginner through the first few months of training quite comfortably because I had been reflecting and learning about the sport constantly throughout the year.

23. Nag People

"If you don't go after what you want, you'll never have it. If you don't ask, the answer is always no." - Nora Roberts

In Denmark, my nagging was shameless. Poor Per (my group's coach) hardly got a minute's peace and quiet without me asking him questions or trying to twist his arm to give me an extra 15 minutes of multiball so that I could work on something I was particularly struggling with.

Normally I feel bad about this kind of thing – I'm very British I guess and don't like to be pushy – but in these kind of situations I feel like the coaches kind of enjoy it. They like to feel wanted and they love coaching players that are keen and passionate about table tennis.

Coaches and more experienced players have so much knowledge that they could share with you, but they aren't just going to walk around preaching it all day long. You need to go up and ask them questions. The kids that are confident enough to pester the older players are usually the ones who come out on top in the end.

24. Get Over The Fear Of Looking Stupid

"If you are not willing to look stupid, nothing great is ever going to happen to you." - Dr. Gregory House

There were multiple times during the year where I reckon I

looked really stupid. The worst was probably doing shadow play in my local gym with Ben shouting out random shots and me having to move and play them. Everyone else in the gym was doing normal stuff; free weights, running, cycling. I was playing imaginary table tennis. Ben even made me do it with my bat in my hand in front of the floor-to-ceiling mirror.

That was a good thing for me to be doing in terms of improving my table tennis, but I still looked like a fool doing it. There are loads of these – things you probably should do but don't because you don't want to look stupid.

One is doing a warm up before a match at a tournament, or even worse, at a local league match. Nobody else seems to warm up by jogging, sidestepping and skipping around the table etc. That means, if you do, you look like a right plonker. "Who's this guy taking it so serious?", people are thinking to themselves. Everyone would play better if they did a warm up, but you feel like you can't because nobody else does. Ultimately, you just need to accept the fact there are going to be times when you look a bit stupid but it's the right thing to do.

25. Don't Compare Yourself To Others

"I generally find that comparison is the fast track to unhappiness. No one ever compares themselves to someone else and comes out even. Nine times out of ten, we compare ourselves to people who are somehow better than us and end up feeling more inadequate." - Jack Canfield

Every time we visited Swerve I would be comparing myself to ten-year-old George. I knew we had started playing at pretty much the same time as each other so I wanted to know how good he was and if I looked better than him. I'd certainly been outworking him so it seemed completely unfair if he was better than me.

The thing is; nothing good can come from comparing yourself to others. If you come up short you can start doubting yourself, worrying that you lack 'talent', and wondering what is so special about the other player. If it looks like you are doing better than others you can easily become complacent, believing that table tennis comes naturally to you, and you don't need to work as hard as these other suckers. It's lose-lose.

The best attitude to have is one of respect for your fellow players and a desire to keep improving yourself, regardless of how everyone else is doing. I couldn't control how quickly George was improving and worrying about keeping up with him was a waste of time. All I could do was give my best and accept whatever results that brought.

26. Act Like A Professional

"You can't get much done in life if you only work on the days when you feel good." - Jerry West

Something else I learnt in Denmark (and from Steve Brunskill in Middlesbrough) was the importance of acting like a professional – even if you aren't. That isn't to say you should start copying the professionals and trying to play shots like them (that didn't work) but look at their habits, tendencies, attitudes and professionalism and mimic it.

For example, professional players take their time in between points. This allows them to collect their thoughts and plan what they want to do in the next point. Most amateur players rush through games in twice the speed of the professionals. It would be wise to act like a professional and take your time when serving, even if your opponent isn't. Professional players also take full advantage of the towel breaks every six points.

It would be wrong to think that professional players

started doing these things after they got good. No – these professional habits are what helped them to become great players in the first place. They are professionals because they have professional habits.

Professional players also practice every day. After all, it's their job. But there must be plenty of days when they don't feel like practicing, but they do it anyway. It's about turning up and doing the work whether you want to or not. That is a professional.

27. Confidence Is Key

"Optimism is the faith that leads to achievement. Nothing can be done without hope and confidence." - Helen Keller

Table tennis is a really weird sport. The difference between making a shot and missing it are tiny. You need to have confidence in your shots and confidence in your ability in general.

I remember the immediate improvement I saw after watching Brian Pace's Perfect Forehand Loop video on YouTube. Ultimately, what that video did for me was give me confidence in my forehand loop. Before watching that video, I would always be worrying whether I had the correct bat angle while making my swing. Sometimes I would even try and change it or wimp out of a big shot at the last minute. This self-doubt completely ruined my game. Once I started just swinging through the ball with conviction my game immediately improved.

When it comes to your overall level of confidence, I believe that is largely dependent upon how you picture yourself playing in your mind's eye. Do you see yourself playing your best or making mistakes and doing things wrong? I spent most of the year watching videos of myself and pointing out everything I was doing wrong. As such, my self-confidence was pretty low. Once I started watching my confidence-boosting 'best of' videos that changed completely. I was able to see myself as a competent player, winning points, and playing my own game.

I really enjoyed using video to analyse my performance and improvement, but the lesson here is to make sure you get the balance right. I remember reading somewhere that Jan Ove Waldner didn't like to watch back matches he had underperformed in as he thought it would hurt his self-confidence. Instead, he focused on watching his best matches over and over again.

28. Have Fun!

"Winning is only half of it. Having fun is the other half." - Bum Phillips

Table tennis is fun – or at least it should be. It's important to remember that. Once you start getting competitive and thinking about winning and losing, you can lose some of the initial fun you experienced. Too much hardcore training is another way for table tennis to become a chore.

I remember how I felt towards the end of August when I was completely burned out from overtraining. The fun had gone and I hated table tennis. You need to make sure you don't get to that point. Remember what it is about the sport you enjoy, why you are putting in all this work, and go easy sometimes. There is nothing wrong with having a light season and doing fun drills once in a while.

If you watch any of Jan Ove Waldner's matches, and he had a very long and successful career, you'll see that he knew how to have fun on the table. He was constantly experimenting and trying out new shots. He would sometimes toy with his opponents seemingly for his own amusement.

And when you come off from a crushing defeat, and

you feel like the whole world is against you, remember it is just a game of ping pong. Everybody has ups and downs and you'll be back playing fantastic table tennis before you know it.

29. There Is No Secret

"Hard work and discipline are what you need to succeed. This applies to everything. There really is no secret—or shortcut—that will get you around this. Get to it. Now." - Ian Stewart

We spent a lot of time searching for a shortcut to table tennis expertise. We didn't really find anything. I suggest you don't waste your time doing the same.

It can be tempting to believe that the top table tennis players have unearthed some kind of secret the rest of us are yet to discover. Some people might tell you they know the secret (they're lying), while others will talk about how the Chinese have this secret system that produces top players (which is a little more believable but still not true).

There is no secret, shortcut or hack to becoming an awesome table tennis player. It's about doing the right things, getting in a high quantity and quality of practice, playing loads of matches, gaining experience. If you want to get really good it is going to take you a really long time - the top players in the world have all been playing for twenty years plus – but it is possible.

Start working now and, most importantly, don't quit until you reach your goals.

FURTHER RESOURCES

"Absorb what is useful, reject what is uselesse." - Bruce Lee

All About The Challenge

The website with all of the blog posts and articles that were written during the challenge. Here you can find exactly how we were both feeling and the proof that all the events in this book are accurate. Also on this site you can find details of the Marathon in a Year and BJJ in a Year challenges.

www.experinayear.com

Want To Improve Your Table Tennis?

Ben's website which is constantly being updated with great articles and studies into the physical, technical, tactical and mental skills you'll need to develop in order to achieve success in table tennis.

www.experttabletennis.com

Videos From The Challenge

The YouTube channel where you can find all the videos from the challenge that are referenced in this book.

www.youtube.com/ExpertTableTennis

All The Equipment From The Challenge

After the challenge we were contacted by many people to ask how much the challenge had cost and for advice on what equipment to buy if they wanted to do their own table tennis challenge. All in all Sam spent £3,063 during the year. This post has the complete breakdown including all the equipment he bought.

www.expertinayear.com/cost-to-learn-a-skill/

Feel free to email us at info@expertinayear.com if you have anything you'd like to ask.

Made in the USA
Middletown, DE
17 January 2019